What Others Are Saying about
Becoming Living Stones...

"Whether your brokenness seems insignificant or insurmountable, you are worth the time and attention, because your healing and restoration await." I could stop right there. That sentence alone is worth reading *Becoming Living Stones.*

First-hand testimonies are normally the hardest but are the most genuine because they derive from wisdom born of first-hand knowledge. Denae's testimony shows us the importance of seeking out personal healing and restoration in order to victoriously emerge in the identity we were each created for.

Her courageous journey will motivate you to visit the pain of hindrances that hold you captive and prevent you from believing in who you truly are. If you are stuck somewhere in life, especially in the pain of any brokenness, and want to become a living testament of healing, I recommend *Becoming Living Stones* to you.

TRISHA FROST,
AUTHOR, *EXPERIENCING THE FATHER'S EMBRACE THROUGH LOSS AND GRIEF: FINDING UNBROKEN COURAGE IN TIMES OF CRISIS*
CO-FOUNDER, SHILOH PLACE MINISTRIES

A mom never wants to read about her child's pain, but to read my daughter Denae's story and see where God has brought her today is what every praying par

What message could be tir us to look within and admit we are headed? *Becoming Living Ston* ho has found themselves in a mess, living in fear with everything falling to pieces around them.

I am so proud of Denae and her walk with God! So thankful God gave us a miracle; she was born! She is such a joy to all who connect with her. As you read, your life too can be changed. You too will become a living stone!

ROSELLA ANGEL RIDINGS, MOM OF DENAE HAAS
PRESIDENT, RIDINGS MINISTRIES INTERNATIONAL
FOUNDER, METRO HOPE FOR KIDS
PASTOR AND MISSIONARY

Becoming Living Stones is a powerful testimony of someone who has walked through her own pain and found the love and grace of Jesus that always brings healing. Denae shares her journey to wholeness and personal revelation of God's goodness with honesty and vulnerability. This book is a beautiful reminder that our good Father wants us to walk free from fear and shame. Denae leads the reader to receive and experience the Lord's forgiveness as she shares her own journey. *Becoming Living Stones* will encourage and strengthen you in your own walk with the Lord and will be a tool to help you minister healing to others.

MICHELLE HASWELL, AUTHOR, *LIVING REFRESHED, EMPOWERING WOMEN WITH TOOLS FOR LEADERSHIP*
CO-PASTOR, NORTHLANDS CHURCH

I've watched Denae (Ridings) Haas grow from a delightful girl into an awesome woman of God! *Becoming Living Stones* is an amazing demonstration of the anointing on her gift as a wordsmith! I enjoyed reading it, and I highly recommend this book for individuals and group Bible studies!

HENRY E. KINSEY, PASTOR AND MISSIONARY
KING'S KIDS MINISTRY/MINISTERIOS HIJOS DEL REY

It's easy to get caught up in the stresses of our day-to-day and miss living for what matters most. Denae Haas's powerful book *Becoming Living Stones* will motivate, inspire, and equip you to live your life today in ways that will impact eternity for you and others.

CORY TRUBE, SMALL GROUP COORDINATOR
DESTINY WORSHIP CENTER (PCB)

If you are unsatisfied with your spiritual life as it is, this book is for you. Through Denae's insights you will undergo a life-changing transformation to become who God created you to be. *Becoming Living Stones* is a great tool to use as you journey alone or with friends.

JOY STRANG, CFO
CHARISMA MEDIA

Having known Denae for most of her life, I have witnessed God's faithfulness to fulfill the joy and purpose for which she was created! She is a gifted author and teacher, and we congratulate her for sharing her story, which is anointed with truth and love. A perfect balance of personal testimony and God's Word!

They overcame by the blood of the Lamb and by the word of their testimony. —Revelation 12:11 KJV

Becoming Living Stones is an intimate testimony that inspires renewed purpose and healing of the heart. This beautifully composed instructive work is caring and gentle, convicting and humbling. There is healing and empowering inside this journey to true love and freedom. We are habitations of the very Spirit of God! We are living stones!

Becoming Living Stones is perfect for individuals and small groups.

DR. HAYWARD L. MILLER AND DIANNE MILLER, MA, EDS
LIVING WORD CHURCH

Becoming Living Stones is a book that every follower of Christ should read. Watching Denae's faith journey unfold from brokenness and fear to complete surrender to the Father, I have both witnessed and shared the fruit of her walk with the Lord that led her to write this book. Her vulnerability and transparency make me proud. God will use it to transform many lives—including yours!

JOHN HAAS, DIRECTOR OF OPERATIONS/OWNER
LAGUNA BEACH CHRISTIAN RETREAT

BECOMING LIVING STONES

— Come Alive —
to Who You Were Made to Be

BECOMING LIVING STONES

— Come Alive —
to Who You Were Made to Be

DENAE HAAS

HIGHERLIFE
PUBLISHING & MARKETING
OVIEDO, FL

HigherLife Publishing & Marketing
P.O. Box 623307
Oviedo, FL 32762
AHigherLife.com

Cover and interior artwork by Jill DeHaan
Back cover photo by Gabby Champagne Media

ISBN Paperback: 978-1-954533-21-9
ISBN Ebook: 978-1-954533-22-6
LOC # 1-10343883051

Printed in the United States

10 9 8 7 6 5 4 3 2 1

This book is dedicated to the people of Destiny Worship Center in Panama City Beach, FL, who have walked alongside me and my family. They've shown us what it looks like to live honestly and to wholeheartedly follow Jesus, and I am forever grateful.

Contents

Section Three
The Tools—Filled and Empowered

Section Four
The Robe—A New Life

Introduction

What a beautiful home, God-of-the-Angel-Armies!
I've always longed to live in a place like this, always
dreamed of a room in your house, where I could sing
for joy to God-alive!

—Psalm 84:1–2 the message

WHEN WE FIND THAT trusting in ourselves has fallen short, and when the making of our own lives has left rubble all around, then it's time to look at the weak and broken places. It's time to consider a safer place to dwell. Considering your inner life—your thoughts, memories, and beliefs—are you living in peace and confidence, or do fear and insecurity rule? Are any areas impaired, stunted, and holding you back? Are you held in cycles that are preventing you from becoming a joyful dwelling place for God?

We all have places of fallout and our own collection of debris. The question is, have you become desperate enough, yet, to do something about it?

If your thoughts are often troubled and you believe you're broken, yet you want to be mended, to know real peace and to live

Whether your brokenness seems insignificant or insurmountable your healing and restoration await.

in freedom, then this book is for you. Whether your brokenness seems insignificant or insurmountable your healing and restoration await. You are worth the time and attention. Come and find that the Lord truly is close to the brokenhearted. Draw near and find His acceptance and rest. Come close and know God as your security and most tender Savior as your broken heart is mended, your mind is renewed, and your fractured life becomes whole.

The Lord allows us to do things our own way, if that's what we choose. He gives us the choice of making our own home, building our own sort of Tower of Babel and giving ourselves a name. Choosing independence from our Maker's hand, one can form bricks and build a life apart from Him. But when a moment of breaking comes, when the pieces become brittle and start to fall apart, we see that our own way leads to dissatisfaction and destruction. This falling down holds great purpose. Humbled and hungry, we become willing to face our fears. We become willing to acknowledge our need.

In my own brokenness, fear ruled my thoughts, darkened my perception, and dictated my behavior. Fear had followed me for most of my life. It held me captive and kept me from becoming my Father's design. Yet when I faced the possibility of losing one of my adult children to a dangerous lifestyle, fear grew to overshadow everything else. I'd tried all I could to rescue them, and I was desperate to find a solution. But, my many tears, pleading, and even manipulation all fell short of making an impact. When some of my greatest fears came true, my foundation started to shake. I had believed in myself—had faith in my own understanding and strength, yet when pressed, I fell short.

Held against a wall by a mindset of fear, I finally faced the truth that I wasn't enough. I wasn't enough to save my child, and I wasn't enough to hold my own self secure. This great pressing and ultimate breaking were a part of God's design. He used it all to begin the process of uncovering my hurting places because He wanted to bring healing. He wanted to restore me into His original design. The Lord used my weakness to show me that I needed Him, so He could reveal Himself safe and strong. He got my attention so I'd allow Him to restore and rebuild my life. His restoration would come through knowing Him and being known *by Him*. Through my breaking came surrender, and that's when God came close and showed me what true love looks like. He showed me that He's a faithful Father, a constant Guide, and the safe shelter that I desperately needed.

To transform me into a place where He dwells, and to transform your life too, the Lord gave me a vision. It came a few years after fully surrendering my life to Him, when He began to heal my wounded heart. This vision and the revelation that has unfolded since has brought clarity to the process of finding freedom from the grip of fear by learning to trust in God and allowing Him to build my life. In the discovery, I've found that He is kind, and He is faithful, and He always has something incredible in mind. This message trades worry and fear for trust and belief. It enables us to become something new. It holds an offer of great exchange for anyone who will choose to say yes.

In this vision, I was standing beside a broken-down wall that had once surrounded and protected a city. It was an old stone wall that had been badly breached. Broken pieces laid scattered around the ground. The image led me to study the book of Nehemiah, in which I found people living inside their own broken-down wall. They'd been ravaged and stolen from, left defenseless, vulnerable, and exposed. Their enemy could return anytime without warning and continue the assault, so they lived in unrest, weighed down by fear. Restrained by the shame of insecurity, they were unable to live confidently in freedom, so they were unable to fully glorify God. In his book titled *Victorious Christian Service, Studies in the Book of Nehemiah*, Alan Redpath further explains the severity of their depravity:

> The fact that the city which had once been the center of God's dealings with His people lay in ruins was not merely a reproach to them, it was a reproach to the honor and to the name of their God. That was to be the inspiration and the power behind all this work of revival. It was not simply a disgrace to them; it was a shame to Him. (44)

Living in shame was not what the Father had planned for His children. Nehemiah 1:3 explains, "They said to me, 'Those who survived the exile and are back in the province are in great trouble and disgrace. The wall of Jerusalem is broken down, and its gates have been burned with fire'" (NIV). There was no wall of protection, so they couldn't freely live as children of God who had been rescued and restored. Fear kept them restrained.

They had left God as their first love and disobeyed His commands, given for their benefit. They'd gone their own way and removed themselves from His guidance and protection. Yet, when they realized their need and returned, the Lord was faithful to receive and restore them. In spite of their rebellion, God promised if they came back, they would know Him as their shelter once again. He said, "but if you have a change of heart and return to Me and walk according to My commands, then no matter how far you have gone, even to the places beyond the horizon, I will gather you and bring you to the place of My choosing, where My very name dwells" (Neh. 1:9 THE VOICE).

Just like the people without protection, the ones who'd wandered away and needed to return, I had moved outside of the Lord's presence of protection and lived in a land of fear. Hindered by doubt and distrust, my foundation lacked His strength and peace. I had prioritized my comfort and the people around me and trusted in myself more than I trusted in God. Not honoring Him as my dwelling place was a betrayal to the Lord because the covenant we shared meant something to Him. He was completely devoted, but my heart was divided, like a wife who was unfaithful. I didn't know how much I needed the protection of His arms. I didn't realize how much I needed His perfect love. But brokenness taught me.

> *Jealous for my love, He longed for me to really know Him and to be known by Him so we could share a real relationship—the kind that's close and built on trust.*

He loved me too much to leave me in ruins, living in fear, and bearing life's heavy burdens apart from Him. Jealous for my love, He longed for me to really know Him and to be known by Him so we could share a real relationship—the kind that's close and built on trust. He wanted to be my place of protection and peace, so I could rely on His strength. Instead of prioritizing people and things over Him and fearfully trying to control, He wanted me to choose Him first and to trust Him with my life, as well as the ones I loved. The Lord wanted me to have peace with who He made me to be, to keep becoming and to enjoy the free and generous life that He'd given. He wanted me to receive His limitless love and to freely, joyfully give it away. The plans He designed just for me, He wanted to help me fulfill.

God uses our brokenness to reveal how much we need Him. Humbled, we start to rightly see who He really is, how greatly He loves, and who He's made us to be. When we turn to Him in meekness, He deals with us kindly. Although He is gentle, He's also strong enough to guard us against every attack. It's up to you and me to return to Him wholeheartedly, to stop giving the enemy entry by abiding in the arms of Jesus and trusting in God alone. Now is the time to make the One who made you your strong and sure Foundation and find your identity in Him. Now is the time to secure yourself in intimacy and fully commit to your covenant with the Lord. It's time to trust in God.

During my vision of the broken-down wall, time progressed, and I was given four things. Each item, given one at a time, represents a piece of the process for becoming a dwelling place for the Lord.

The first thing I received was a brick. It represents the things that make up and influence our lives—our experiences, beliefs, and understandings. In the first section, we'll come clean about our brokenness and receive restoration. We'll examine our hearts and minds and look closely at what we believe in. Lies will be exposed and removed as our hearts are healed and we receive the truth. We'll return to our First Love and come under God's protection by trusting in Him as our continual Creator.

The next element was a loaf of bread. It represents the nourishment that Jesus is and gives. In the second section, we'll seek to know the Lord more and learn to better receive from Him. We'll partake in His life and be restored, fed, and sustained by making Him our priority and participating in the daily practices that lead us to life. This living bread will mature and strengthen us for the work of being made into a beautiful place where the Lord loves to reside.

Next, I was given a spade for setting the bricks and sealing in the gaps. In our own strength, we're weak and lacking, so we need to be filled and empowered with God's Spirit—His very presence, and all that He has to give. While being rebuilt, we'll use the spiritual tools He provides, to effectively resist the enemy. In section three, we'll learn to remain in Jesus and be led by the Holy Spirit as we employ the tools given for warfare. We'll continue to grow strong while we defend *and* take back stolen ground!

The last gift and piece of the process was a white robe. It was laid over my arm, gently given to represent the new life that is ours, by believing in Jesus, and simply putting on all that He has to give. In this fourth and final section, we'll put on the robes of righteousness that enable us to be loved by the Lord and to love like He does. We'll wear His gifts and present our lives like a crown to our King.

Together, we will face our fears and come to trust in the Lord. We'll get to know Him intimately and appreciate His gifts, as we receive ongoing transformation into His original design. Filled and empowered with His Spirit, we'll fight darkness and defend our territory. We will know God as our First Love—our empowering protector, provision, and peace. Along the way, we will freely become something incredible that houses the very presence of God!

We no longer have to stay stuck in our old ways. While we're still surrounded by the mess that we've made, the Lord is breaking down walls and bringing us back to Him. He waits for our return, ready to forgive and demonstrate His compassion and unfailing love. He is waiting for the moment we will say yes to wholehearted devotion, because that's when our adventure with Him begins! At this pivotal point, when we feel like we're at our worst and at the end of our rope, if we'll let go, we'll find that we're actually at a beautiful beginning!

In my own despair and living within a broken-down wall, the Lord came to me and proved that He was faithful. He found me in the rubble and led me out. When I returned and committed to Him as my Lord and center of my life He began to restore me into the girl He originally designed. As I learned to trust and cooperate with Him in relationship, He began to reconstruct my life. This time, I was being built upon the strong and perfect foundation of Jesus Christ. His Presence has become what I live for.

The Lord longs for us all to return to Him and promises that when we seek Him with our whole heart we will find Him (Jer. 29:13). This means we release our own ideas and understandings and fully yield to Him with an undivided heart. As we make Christ alone our Foundational Stone and allow Him to build our lives upon Himself, He will restore our brokenness and satisfy every bit of hunger. *He* will make us into something stunning. We have a part to play and decisions to make.

Where is it that you're dwelling? Do you live in a place of safety and peace, or do fear and trouble rule? It's time to return to your First Love. It's time for your heart to be healed by Love Himself. It's time to be made strong and set upon the solid foundation of the Lord. It's time to catch a vision of what it will look like to live fully known and loved, restored and surrounded by peace, and protected and armed for defense. Are you ready to be free and filled with God's presence? Our ultimate goal is to live

> *It's time to return to your First Love. It's time for your heart to be healed by Love Himself.*

encompassed by the very One who loves us best and makes restoration possible. He is the One who has enabled us to experience a life of unlimited peace and security. He is the One who has given us victory and made us something new. We need to learn to believe it!

It's time to begin the restoration and the rebuilding. If you choose to enter in, as you move through the book, there will be opportunity to respond at the end of each chapter through *Meditation* and *Prayer*. Meditate on truth so it can permeate deep within, and respond in prayer to solidify, agree with, and declare what the Lord is saying to you.

The Lord is ready to listen and guide, as we welcome Him into His rightful place and include Him in our daily lives. As we respond, He'll continue to speak through His Word, through others, in thoughts or visions, impressions, dreams, books, or in any number of creative ways! I expect Him to speak to you through the words of this book. Be open to hearing and ready to receive. Expect it—even wait until you do.

As you're obedient to the Lord's leading and remain faithful to the work at hand, you'll become a life that Jesus can entrust Himself to—one that He finds faithful and fully devoted to His heart. This will be a completely different kind of life. You will love and trust God. You will know God intimately and stay close to Him. Loosed from the grip of fear, you will freely live with purpose and without shame. In appreciation for the One who saved and set you free, you will live open-hearted and open-handed—generously giving back to God and the people He brings into your life. What joy of discovery awaits as you become who you truly are. You will awaken to incredible dreams and partner with God to fulfill the plans that He's designed just for you. You will find and take your place in the Body of Christ and grow strong through connection. You'll also learn how to receive rest, abundant joy, and peace, even amid life's difficulty, because you'll be dwelling within the perfect Presence of Jesus.

There are so many truths waiting to be discovered and much work to be done, so let us begin this adventure of *becoming a living stone—a dwelling place for God.*

> **Now may the God of peace—who brought up from the dead our Lord Jesus, the great Shepherd of the sheep, and ratified an eternal covenant with his blood—may he equip you with all you need for doing his will. May he produce in you, through the power of Jesus Christ, every good thing that is pleasing to him. All glory to him forever and ever! Amen.**
>
> **—HEBREWS 13:20–21**

SECTION 1:
THE BRICK
The Work Begins Within

> They said to me, "Things are not going well for those who returned to the province of Judah. They are in great trouble and disgrace. The wall of Jerusalem has been torn down, and the gates have been destroyed by fire."
>
> —NEHEMIAH 1:3

WHEN WE EXPERIENCE DIFFICULTY that shakes the walls of our hearts and leaves our foundations exposed, it's an opportunity to notice the hurts that lie below the surface. It's an opportunity to look at what our lives have been built upon and examine their effect. The Lord allows this shaking to reveal the truth. He offers us a way that's better than our own and a foundation that will stand no matter what we encounter. There is no damage too great or wound too deep that He cannot heal. If we'll choose to humble ourselves and respond with a surrendered and obedient heart, God will remove the things that hinder our lives and repair every breach, one by one.

The Lord knows everything about us; He is fully aware of our past, present, and future. He knows of the hardships instigated by darkness, designed to bring us harm. Some of these hardships happened when we were just a child. Some came as a result of the way we chose to respond. Others happened because of our deliberate disobedience. We don't always understand why the Lord allows these difficult things, but we can trust that He is in control and working all things out for our good—even our own poor choices. Remember Romans 8:28: "And we know that God causes everything to work together for the good of those who love God and are called according to his purpose for them." He is working for our good. The Lord is faithful and aware, and nothing is ever wasted. He will use every bit of the pain and the testing to soften and purify our hearts and to renew our minds, if we will allow it.

> *There is no damage too great or wound too deep that He cannot heal.*

We can stay the same, if we'd like. We can choose to pretend that we don't have pain and continue to live with broken-down walls, remaining afflicted with hurt and burdened by fear. But there's an invitation for healing and transformation. Let's heed the words of Nehemiah, "You see the bad situation we are in, that Jerusalem is desolate and its gates have been burned by fire. Come, let's rebuild the wall of Jerusalem so that we will no longer be a reproach" (Neh. 2:17 NASB). If we're willing, we can yield to the process of restoration and build a better legacy. We can truly pass through these trials and become healed and strong.

We can learn new things and grow into the original daughter or son that our Creator designed us to be. If we'll choose to humbly cooperate then dead things like selfishness, pride, and unforgiveness can be cut away, and our new lives can emerge. This is our opportunity to become a beautiful dwelling place for God! Let's respond like those listening to Nehemiah, "Then they said, 'Let us arise and build.' So they put their hands to the good work" (Neh. 2:18 NASB). The Lord is offering us this fresh start. Let's open our hearts and take it!

Chapter One

Assessing the Damage

You can buy two sparrows for only a copper coin, yet
not even one sparrow falls from its nest without the
knowledge of your Father. Aren't you worth much
more to God than many sparrows? So don't worry.
For your Father cares deeply about even the smallest
detail of your life.

—MATTHEW 10:29–31 TPT

WITH THE SHAKING OF foundation, let's take the opportunity to deal with the hurts that lie deeper below.
We've all experienced emotional wounds inflicted upon us by
the hurtful words and actions of those that we love the most.
Questions like, *What's wrong with you?* leave an imprint. Shame
marks us with the disapproving looks, the jokes, and the sense
that we're not enough. Although our parents, teachers, and
friends may not have intended to cause us long-lasting damage with their teasing, shaming, or rejection, the messages we've
heard while growing up often leave us feeling less than acceptable. Even in the best of families there is brokenness.

When left unhealed, our pain festers and creates an opening
for the enemy to deposit lies about our identity and self-worth.
If we ignore our injuries, hoping they'll fade away, then we'll

continue to carry the pain and keep believing the false things the enemy has whispered about us. We will continue to live and react from a wounded place, while undoubtedly trying to convince ourselves and everyone else that we're really okay. But if we aren't all right deep down, the wound will eventually show. Whether it manifests as anger or frustration, insecurity, jealousy, or any other negative response, instead of bringing relief, it only heaps on more shame and leaves us feeling more alone. Instead of covering up, let's step into the opportunity to bravely assess the damage, so healing can finally come.

Although it was fear for my adult child that screamed loud enough to get my attention, the Lord used it as an opportunity to begin the process of looking within and becoming honest with myself. On one of my most fear-filled days, I repeatedly called the rehab facility where my child was checked in. So very desperate and afraid, I was trying my best to understand and control and fix the situation. To be honest, I was not prepared when the woman on the other end of the line asked me what was going on—with me. She called me out on my fearful behavior and encouraged *me* to get help and support. I was so used to putting my attention on my child that I had missed my own behavior. I had missed how afraid *I* really was.

Pride had long held me back from being one who'd come clean and admit any need. But in this place of pressing, I began to realize the truth as I confessed that I was scared and also felt unworthy of my pain. It was the first time I spoke of my fear and inadequacy honestly. Simple, but profound truth came to me through a stranger that day as she explained that all hurt hurts and *all* pain is painful. I'd barely met her, but her honest words gave me permission to feel the fear and the pain that had been building up for so long.

The pride that had kept me bound to secrecy and shame had to take a back seat as I took her advice and stepped into Celebrate Recovery, a place of support where believers can be open and honest about their deficiencies. That's where I first spoke of my fears. I let my tears fall with complete strangers and felt embraced by their warmth and acceptance. They walked around comfortable in their imperfect skin and showed me what it

> *Bravely beginning to admit the truth was so life-giving that it unlocked a deeper desire for more truth and more freedom.*

looked like to live free. Bravely beginning to admit the truth was so life-giving that it unlocked a deeper desire for more truth and more freedom.

With their help, I became willing to slow down and see things as they really were, deep inside my own heart. What I saw when I looked within were wounds that I'd carried around for years, thick scars that whispered, *You're not enough. You should be different. You're not acceptable as you are.* What I saw was a fearful forty-something who struggled to know who she truly was. I saw that I needed to say yes to the opportunities of honesty the Lord was offering to me because I so longed to be free. With brave believers who'd walked this way before showing me the way, I pulled aside and allowed the Lord to begin to do the work on my heart.

I'd spent the formative years of my life watching my parents take their place on a field of sorts, shepherding the sheep and bringing in the harvest of the broken and the lost. Growing up a pastor's child gave me a front-row seat to the church. I watched without knowing how to find my place.

There was so much movement, always work to be done, and I was carried along with a pressure to do and say the right things as I tried to stay afloat on the quickly moving waters. I often vacillated between wanting to please and playing the rebellious pastor's daughter. People were fickle and I'm sure everyone in my house—my mom, dad, and me—all felt the strain. I wanted to be accepted just as me. I wanted it to be okay for me to try out and see who I really was. I wanted to know I had a place apart from what I could do for the church. It was just hard to find. My experience affected my beliefs. Although I knew I was loved, I believed on my own, apart from my family and their work for the Lord, I was a let-down and lacked value. I wasn't a natural doer, so I believed that I had nothing of worth to give.

As a child, I would sit on our brown carpet watching *Mr. Roger's Neighborhood*. There was something so appealing, so accepting in his demeanor. He slowed down and spoke to children with kindness and care. He didn't brush them off as something unimportant because they couldn't contribute in obvious ways. No, he seemed to look into the child and see their value and the unique worth that each one held. He looked until he saw who they really were, and he honored them there. Even though parents try to love well and do the best that they can, don't we all need the deep, accepting Mr. Rogers' kind of love, the kind that sees and values the true child, apart from anything we do?

In reality and apart from a dreamy, perfectly presented TV kind of love, what I really needed was to know that God had a special place in His heart just for me. I needed to know that He had a specific plan for that lost girl, but I just couldn't see it. I thought I had to earn my way and I didn't know how. The feeling of being unacceptable deep within created a void. The enemy was waiting and deftly deposited lies. Through my bitterness and belief, they stuck. Darkness suggested that I was like a shadow with nothing of worth to say. The enemy whispered that others didn't really know me, didn't want to know me, and that I wasn't worth knowing anyway. It felt like I was on the outside looking in, like I didn't belong and my voice couldn't be heard. Believing I was unacceptable and growing detached from my own self, I suffered from the shame of insecurity.

What a dirty word, *shame*. It lurked like an undercurrent, always running underneath. Aware of its presence, I covered it up with my own remedy of pride and put on a brave face because that's what I thought good Christians were supposed to do. That's what I had seen believers do. We didn't show our scars; we didn't let others in on the pain. People were uncomfortable and uninterested in that. And to top it off, I knew others had experienced things far worse than me. So, I swallowed it down, smoothed out my dress, and put on a smile as shame whispered, *Who are you to feel pain?* I'd been loved and lived in a warm home with a good family, so I agreed—*What right do I have to hurt?*

My experiences not only affected my beliefs about myself, but they also impacted the way that I saw God. I believed He expected perfection and preferred people who did the right things more often than I did. Surely, He must be constantly disappointed with me. I thought He was more interested in what I could do for Him than He was interested in me. I believed His love was conditional, based on my actions. I thought it was limited like the love of people, like the ones who withdrew and withheld when I failed to meet their expectations or caused disappointment.

Knowing my flaws and limitations, I knew there was no way I could measure up to God's high expectations. Instead of simply acknowledging my fears and inadequacy to my Creator, I held it in and hid it away. I didn't trust God to love me just as I was. He had so much acceptance, love, and purpose to give, but as long as I hid behind fear and shame and believed the enemy's lies, I resisted receiving God's love and letting it all the way in. My distrust hindered my experience of His love reaching in and meeting my deepest needs.

Years later, when hardships helped me become desperate enough to acknowledge my fear and pain, I traveled to a weekend retreat designed for inner healing. Time spent there with patient believers helped me identify my brokenness and beliefs. Together, we began to unwind the religious lies and false expectations away from God's true character. I'm still unravelling them. But I finally found safety within the body of Christ to honestly face what I was feeling. Because of their time and care, I realized that God never wanted me to pretend. He didn't expect me to do anything apart from Him. And He never wanted me to be anything but honest.

Unsure and uncomfortable, I admitted I was hurt and wasn't ready to forgive. And although I was revealing I was flawed and had need, it was okay. They didn't shame or scold me; they allowed me to be honest and stayed there with me, encouraging with love and truth. They helped me find healing by leading me to the heart of Jesus. I discovered there that He wanted me to take the mask off. Jesus was okay with me not being okay.

While in worship that weekend, I felt Jesus very near. One morning the presence of the Holy Spirit was hovering in the room, thick and heavy. God was offering me an opportunity to bring my need for acceptance and a perfect parent's love directly to Him. I sensed His face close to mine, really looking and allowing me to mourn the pain. I found true the words of Jesus, "God blesses those who mourn, for they will be comforted" (Matt. 5:4). His eyes were looking, seeing the real me. He was looking at my loneliness and longing, and He let me know that I was loved. From within I heard Him say, "You are not a shadow. *I* see you! And *I delight* in seeing you." He was smiling warmly, and His approval descended deep down into the very core of my childlike being. His love went so far in that I actually believed it.

> *From within I heard Him say, "You are not a shadow. I see you! And I delight in seeing you."*

Experiencing His presence and acceptance enabled me to receive His love. As I released the lie that I was unacceptable and unworthy of being seen and loved as just me, like a black-bird, darkness flapped its wings and flew away. In its place, the Lord gave me the light of His acceptance and undying love. Seen and known by Him, I found my place within His heart. There, I caught a glimpse of the girl I really was—the secure, happy, and trusting childlike daughter He'd created me to be. I began to hope for her return.

What value is found in looking within.

Have you, like me, put on a brave face? Have you covered your wounds and kept them hidden from yourself and the One who loves you most? You must fight the lying undercurrent that pulls you into hiding and drowns you in fear. Stop the torment from the enemy who wants to keep you bound to the pain and living in shadows. Listen to the Lord; He wants you to let down the walls you've hidden behind and allow Him to come near. It won't take Him long to locate the wound and tend to the pain if you're willing to look. What is just underneath the surface, causing disruption and pain, affecting your life? The Lord sees it and He is ready to bring healing. He is ready to uproot the lie and give you His lifegiving light in its place.

It can be frightening to reopen an old injury, but if it's still tender it's not yet healed. If it causes a reaction inside when the memory's brought up, it still needs the Lord's gaze. It's time to unwrap the fear and hold your brokenness before the Lord. This is the first move toward experiencing healing within and to setting things straight. Yes, it will hurt, but it will also be okay. Jesus is waiting for you to become willing to look inside and allow Him to bring truth and transformation to the pain and the lies.

He doesn't want you to pretend that your hurt doesn't hurt. He died so you and I could *really* be healed. Think about that for a minute. All that Jesus went through in His life and on the Cross was not only for our healing on the outside, but grace upon grace, it was for our healing within. He longs to restore us to the original child that the Father dreamed of and created us to be.

If we can picture our hopeful child-like self waiting to be welcomed, nurtured, and valued then it will help us to admit the truth. It will help us remember that we're worth the trouble. As we bravely open our hearts before the Lord, we'll find that the One who is perfect Love is already near. His eyes are smiling, His voice reassuring, *I see you. I love you. And I take great delight in you, just as you are!*

Meditate

Take this moment to get quiet and ask the Lord to help you look at the wound that He would like to heal.

What lie did the enemy deposit after the affliction?

What do you hear Jesus saying? What truth is He giving you in its place?

Listen.

Prayer

Father,

Like David, I want Your truth to come in, so I pray, "I know that you delight to set your truth deep in my spirit. So come into the hidden places of my heart and teach me wisdom" (Psa. 51:6 TPT). Reveal the lies I've believed because of the pain. Thank You for healing me from the inside out.

Show me Your truth and let it fill me. Begin to restore me to who You designed me to be. I'm listening for Your voice.

Thank You for seeing me and loving me just as I am.

I love You too.

Chapter Two

Learning to Trust through Surrender

God blesses those who are poor and realize their need for him, for the Kingdom of Heaven is theirs.

—MATTHEW 5:3

AS WE TAKE THE courageous first step of admitting we need help and healing, we may wonder deep down if God is someone we can truly trust with our heart. From our beginnings, we've been impacted by a world of people who are flawed and broken, people just like you and me. Hurt and disappointments build up, and our natural reaction to the lingering pain is to distrust and pull away. So, we build walls to keep the hurt places safely hidden. But there comes a time when we need to care enough for ourselves that we come out of hiding. There comes a time to open the doors of our hearts completely and invite our Savior and His light all the way in.

Be prepared, there will be a great struggle as the pride of self-reliance tries to "protect us" and obstruct the way. There will be an ongoing battle between the spirit and the will. What's required to win is simple, but it is not easy. What's required is surrender—a complete opening of the door. Then the Lord will lead from there. As we let go of trying to control, and admit that we need our Savior's help, immediately we'll find Him close. We'll find that He's strong enough to shoulder our burdens and wise enough to lead us out. In the humility of surrender, we will discover that God can be trusted and is kind enough to give us the time needed to tend to our hearts.

When we don't trust the Lord, the One who made us and was meant to father and lead us, then we keep Him at arm's length, questioning His motives and ways of doing things, often asking *why* when things don't work out the way we want. Without His intimate influence, His reassurance and wisdom, we pridefully make our own way, crafting our own lives. We follow our own desires, trust our own understanding, and move further and further away from Him.

James 1:14–15 explains, "Temptation comes from our own desires, which entice us and drag us away. These desires give birth to sinful actions. And when sin is allowed to grow, it gives birth to death." Far away, we forget what the Lord is really like. We forget the safety of His securing love and we forget to listen for the wisdom of His voice. The farther away we move, the more tangled we get and the less we trust the One we need the most.

What is the remedy for doubt and distrust? How can we put an end to the cycle of disconnection and disbelief? I believe the answer can be revealed through the song of my story, the one I sing with my life and portray with my words. As a little girl, my family taught me about Jesus, and I loved and believed in Him at a young age. Yet I spent much of my life learning to distrust the Lord. In spite of my dad being a compassionate pastor and my mom faithfully ministering and working beside him, and in spite of growing up falling asleep on church pews and waking up early to take biscuits to the men's morning group with Dad, I grew to distrust the God of the church we loved and labored for.

Further away from unbelief now, I can see my story more clearly. I can easily recall the love I shared with Jesus as a child, a love that was authentic and true. I remember how His presence was always with me, whether I was playing in my little-girl bedroom painted pink, going to church with the people I loved, or jumping on my trampoline in the backyard. Jesus was present in every part of my life and His nearness brought me great joy. His acceptance gave me confidence. His limitless love made me feel safe. With my childlike faith, we shared a simple, yet deeply devoted relationship.

But as I grew out of childhood and into knowing right from wrong, I became resentful of the way the church pulled my family's focus and how it took priority. I felt jealous of the attention that the church received, so I compensated. I made myself feel better by agreeing with pride. I found a sense of entitlement and self-worth through my parents and what they did for God. It gave me value, I thought, and even assumed I was covered with grace because of them. I'd heard the true gospel preached, but somehow I failed to hear the message given in relation to my own heart. I believed in God, loved the memory of Him, yet I couldn't get past my pretense of pride. I couldn't honestly and bravely acknowledge my own need.

As an adult, I convinced myself I was okay by going to church on Sundays and doing my best to be a good Christian, one who knew the right answers and did the right things. I thought I could make my own way as long as I kept doing enough to keep God and the people around me happy. But there was something about what Jesus said in Matthew 7:21–23 that never sat right with me. Every time I heard it, I silently, shamefully wondered if it might apply to me. Jesus declared, "Not everyone who calls out to me, 'Lord! Lord!' will enter the Kingdom of Heaven. Only those who actually do the will of my Father in heaven will enter. On judgment day many will say to me, 'Lord! Lord! We prophesied in your name and cast out demons in your name and performed many miracles in your name.' But I will reply, 'I never knew you. Get away from me, you who break God's laws.'"

I had known the Lord as a child, but I didn't grasp how to really know Him as an adult. In my own strength, I did my best pretending and even fooled myself, as I lived out the truth of Galatians 5:4, "For if you are trying to make yourselves right with God by keeping the law, you have been cut off from Christ! You have fallen away from God's grace." In truth, I neglected our relationship and lacked intimacy with Him. Jesus was not the center of my being, and I wasn't following His way. I refused to humble myself and submit to Christ as my Lord. I just kept thinking that my own strength would be enough. On the outside, I became prideful and judgmental. But on the inside, I was hurt and offended, broken and insecure. Can you relate to any of my story? Have you thought it was up to you to keep up standards, to measure up and prove your worth? Do you think that's what God requires?

I married young, found my own savior in a sense, and tried to keep a firm grip on my life and a watchful eye on the ones I loved. I thought love was my motivation, but deep down, it was fear. I didn't want to lose what I had, so I held on tightly, thinking that's what love looked like. Living on the defense, I was afraid of anything that might threaten my identity or the relationships I valued. When I encountered people that I perceived to hold more value than me it was like being untethered from a secure place and set out to a rocky sea in a one-man boat. It was up to me to keep myself safe and afloat. Insecurity and fear lorded over me. I allowed them to reign.

Fear had been my experience while growing up, too. I'd relied too heavily on others and when they couldn't provide what I needed, I felt alone and afraid. My heart and emotions needed to be divinely protected. I needed to be believed in, even when I wasn't good enough and didn't deserve it. Growing up, when my rebellion felt like rejection to my parents, it caused separation in our relationship. Sometimes, it caused fear to rule. It seemed like it was up to me to find my way.

When it was my turn to be the mother, I was determined not to repeat the pattern of parenting out of fear, but it was what I knew. When my child rebelled, I felt the same fear, felt the same sting of rejection, and reverted back to experience. I tried to lead with love, but in times of turmoil when their choices caused real concern, I defaulted back to the law. I tried to manipulate better behavior by bringing up all the possible terrible consequences that *could happen* instead of staying on my child's side. I spoke to the identity that I saw in the natural, instead of looking to see what God saw and prophesying from that place. I tried to control instead of trusting in God and asking for His help and insight. So I laid down the law, but law laid down doesn't lead any of us to God. Law only causes fear and fear doesn't reach in and move the heart like love does. It manipulates, and in its attempt to control, it does great damage.

Fear and disconnection made me feel defeated as a teen. It made me want to give up and go my own way. I hated that feeling of disconnection and distrust, yet here I was, passing on that same cycle, doing to the child I loved what was done to me.

Fear does not lead one well. Pride lied; it told me I didn't need help with life, that I really wasn't that bad, and if I went to church on Sundays all would be fine. Unbelief whispered that God could not fully be trusted. But when things didn't work out according to plan, things like regrets and broken relationships, my dad suffering from cancer and dying, and my young-adult child seriously struggling, I was left reeling in a whirlwind of insecurity, gripped by fear.

Turns out, the idea of control is a facade. It's a lie to keep us bound to fear, clinging to the people and things we want to hold onto. It keeps us determined to make our own way, trusting in ourselves. It's a false narrative used to keep us questioning the God who made us, unsure of who He designed us to be. Cycling through a lack of identity, insecurity, pride, and fear for years, I finally fell to the bottom, broken. Facing some of my worst fears, the facade of control was shaken away.

The breaking the devil planned to destroy me, and you, the Father in His kindness adapts for our good. Seeing ourselves rightly is humbling, but it helps us acknowledge our need. *We need a Savior.* We need Jesus to be King of our hearts, leader of our lives, and lover of our souls. We need Him to secure us in His heart with His love, to tell us who we are, and to whisper guidance to show us the way. If we want to really learn how to love, we need the Lord to teach us and to help us let go, so we can trust, and rest, and believe Him for the best. In our brokenness, the Lord loves us while envisioning something better, something beautiful. In His persistent pursuit, He sees us as who we *can become*. He sees the *potential* of the love we can share with Him, the special plans He has for you and for me, and the glory we can one day return to Him.

Surrender—the opposite of a proud heart—is what the Lord wants from us all. It's not about performing the outward rituals of going to church or looking clean, it's acknowledging our sin and humbly coming home to His heart, in honesty. In Psalm 51, David wrote, "Going through the motions doesn't please you, a flawless performance is nothing to you. I learned God-worship when my pride was shattered. Heart-shattered lives ready for love don't for a moment escape God's notice" (16-17 THE MESSAGE).

Describing our need to be broken in surrender, Francis Frangipane explains, "This self-sufficiency and self-will is what must break before we can ever fulfill the will of God, which is Christlikeness" (59). In Luke 20:17–18, Jesus refers to Himself as the chief cornerstone, the stone upon which our lives and all of the church is built. Jesus said, "Everyone who falls on that stone will be broken to pieces; but on whomever it falls, it will crush him" (NASB). Frangipane clearly explains our options: "We either fall and break on Christ or He will fall upon us and scatter us like dust" (60).

The Lord allows us to go our own way. He allows us to believe false things about Him and to choose distrust, disobedience, and distance because true love gives freedom of choice. In spite of our rebellion, God never loses sight of us or lets us go. When we repent, we're fully forgiven, washed clean, and able to come in close again. And that's when and where we grow hungry.

God's presence woos us into complete surrender. One summer morning I penned the words in my journal: *I have decided to live by faith.* I was done holding back and ready to give and receive it all. Have you had such a sacred encounter, a marked awakening?

> *When we let go of holding tightly onto our self-built lives, we begin to not only taste, but feast, and see that the Lord is good!*

When we let go of holding tightly onto our self-built lives, we begin to not only taste, but feast, and see that the Lord *is good!* He is good because He's been faithful to you and me and He's never compromised Himself nor His truth. Even at our worst, God never left. He has always stayed the same loving Savior, never gave up, and never let us go. His eyes have always been on you and me and He's held onto the dreams that He has for each of us. We find truth and acceptance not by trying to be good, but by knowing and being known by our Creator. As people who follow Jesus humbly and honesty, we can learn how to read God's Word and listen for His voice and get to know God. The more time we

LEARNING TO TRUST THROUGH SURRENDER

spend with Him, the more we fall in love with the One who has come to our rescue. We owe Him all of our life, all of our love and devotion.

Matthew 5:3–4 explains it perfectly, "You're blessed when you're at the end of your rope. With less of you there is more of God and his rule. You're blessed when you feel you've lost what is most dear to you. Only then can you be embraced by the One most dear to you" (THE MESSAGE). What joy for us in need! When we humble ourselves before the Lord, He heals our brokenness and restores our lives because *He truly loves us*! He loves us more than we've allowed Him to demonstrate. He loves us enough to bring us to a place of brokenness because it is in our brokenness that we find Him.

To trust God is to fully surrender. It's to be yielded and to give Christ first place. It's coming under the Lordship of Jesus and welcoming Him as the Leader of our lives. To trust through surrender is to obey God's ways, even when we don't understand. It's to remember that there is no darkness in Him and that His fatherly intentions for us are pure and good. Our Father God does not want our outward, detached obedience. What does He want? He tells us in Hosea 6:6, "I want you to show love, not offer sacrifices. I want you to know me more than I want burnt offerings." The Lord cares so much more for us than whether or not we follow a list of rules. He has no desire to make us perform or conform to dead, religious ideas. He loves us too much for that. It is truly for *freedom* that Christ set us free! Jesus loosed us from death and darkness, fear and insecurity, so we could live an unbound life with Him—full of love, joy, purpose, and peace. Our response can be like David's,

"Make Zion the place you delight in, repair Jerusalem's broken-down walls. Then you'll get real worship from us, acts of worship small and large, including all the bulls they can heave onto your altar!" (Psa. 51:18–19 THE MESSAGE).

The Lord watches—caring and careful, leading and guiding, smiling and showing us the way to life. He knows that we learn not by pretending, but by living. He's a Father who allows His children to say and do imperfect things and to make mistakes so we can learn and grow. We grow through the good and the bad. And He's okay with our imperfection because He values who we are becoming much more than any pretended persona. In spite of our imperfections, because of His love and the perfect sacrifice of Jesus, when we surrender the Father allows us to come close, and He accepts us, even loves us, just as we are.

In this battle of choosing to surrender, we'll need help; we'll need to rely on the strength of Jesus because Jesus knows surrender. He's shown us what it looks like by living humbly, even though He was God. In spite of being misunderstood by many, Jesus chose to obey the Father and live according to His ways and His plan. Even when He faced death and knew the most consuming darkness was coming, Jesus still surrendered. The night before He took our heaviness and sin on the Cross, Jesus prayed this same prayer three times, "My Father! If it is possible, let this cup of suffering be taken away from me. Yet, I want your will to be done, not mine" (Matt. 26:39). Hold onto these words: *Yet, I want Your will, not mine.* Jesus trusted in the Father's love and faithfulness. He believed something better was on the other side of His surrender and obedience.

Jesus went first. He went before you and faced and won every battle. Now Jesus is reaching out His hand to you, to guide you toward the Cross. Follow His lead, and once there kneel beside Him and release your grip of all the things you've tightly held. You can rest and trust in His strength, His insight, and His perspective. Beside Him, Jesus helps you to pray, to give Him your burdens. His Presence holds you secure, and you're strengthened in His love. There at the Cross with Jesus, you remember what surrender looks like, what it feels like, and you choose to trust.

> *Jesus is reaching out His hand to you, to guide you toward the Cross.*

Learning this lesson of surrender is an ongoing process; it's a letting go and trusting, again and again. Each difficulty is an opportunity to resist the pride of self-reliance and the fear of insecurity and go back to the Cross to humbly acknowledge our need. Each time we kneel, we move to a deeper place of believing and into a more secure place of trust. We reject the pride that says we don't need the Lord's leading and release the lie that suggests we can't trust Him. The day will never come when we find the Father not faithful and good. Yes, we will go through trials. We will go through very difficult and painful things. But the God who created us will never leave us. He will use it all to build us into a strong and purified life.

One day we'll see Him—our Cornerstone, and when we do we want to be shining radiant like gold. When that moment comes, all fear and doubt will be expelled by the glory of His bright light. Until then, until we see Him face to face, we'll find refuge in surrendering wholeheartedly to the Lord at the Cross and abiding in His perfect love. That's where fear cannot exist and where our lives are made whole.

Meditate

Find a quiet place where you can talk to God about trust. Are there any areas that you're holding back?

Picture yourself kneeling in surrender beside Jesus at the Cross. What burdens do you need to release to Him? Remember, His love does not change. Meditate on God's words below and ask Him to fill you with His perfect love. Receive it.

> **Long ago the Lord said to Israel: "I have loved you, my people, with an everlasting love. With unfailing love, I have drawn you to myself."**
>
> —JEREMIAH 31:3

Prayer

Father,

Because of my experiences, I've distrusted You. I've wanted to protect myself and make my own way. Yet, all the while, You've been faithful to me. Help me to trust You more and believe in Your truth. Help me open my heart completely to You and welcome Your love all the way in. Jesus, You send fear running.

I receive Your love.

In Jesus' name, amen.

Chapter Three

Examining Beliefs

Examine yourselves to see if your faith is genuine. Test yourselves.

—2 CORINTHIANS 13:5

W E PUT OUR FAITH in what we believe to be true, and we live our lives based on those beliefs. Our beliefs drive our thinking. They also drive our actions and guide our interactions with God and one another and they color the way we feel about ourselves. The beliefs we put our faith in motivate all we do. As we learn to trust and surrender, why don't we also take inventory of what we're believing? Consider this Proverb, "A person may think their own ways are right, but the Lord weighs the heart" (Prov. 21:2 NIV).

It's the issues of the heart that determine what we believe and how we live. We're in process of becoming more like Christ, but we're not complete yet. We have so much more to learn and many more ways to grow! Because we want to be healthy from the inside out and secured upon the truth, let's test our understandings and look brick by brick, at the ideas influencing our lives. Let's consider their impact and determine what should stay and what should go. Looking at every brick, from the hereditary habits handed down from prior generations to the religious ideas we so quickly defend, let's test each one; get rid of all that's false, and only allow truth to remain.

This ongoing sifting through familiar ground will require an open heart. We'll need to be willing to learn new things. Proverbs 17:16 speaks of the importance of having a teachable heart. It says, "It is senseless to pay to educate a fool, since he has no heart for learning." Let's open our hearts and minds before the Lord and allow Him to help us get to the center of what we believe and why we believe it. He'll help us pinpoint the location of the hurtful experiences that led us to seeing things the wrong way and show us the influences of the world. As healing comes, the false beliefs that slipped in with the pain will be removed. We will receive new understandings and even deepen those we hold true, as they become more closely confirmed and solidified through God's Spirit and His Word.

Let's begin by looking at what makes up our basic foundation of faith. In whose hands have we placed our lives, and ultimately, in whom do we really trust? One night I woke up hearing the words, *It's not faith until you believe.* God's Spirit had whispered the challenging truth right into my heart. I had chosen to live by faith, but there were still some areas of my life in which I didn't really believe God to be good. In Hebrews 11:6 Paul explains, "And it is impossible to please God without faith. Anyone who wants to come to him must believe that God exists and that he rewards those who sincerely seek him." True faith is actually *believing* in who we put our faith in. It's trusting the Lord so much that we stay close to Him and totally rely on His protection and leading.

Ask yourself, "What do I really believe about God? How do I imagine Him to be? Do I see Him rightly, or do I have His true nature tangled up with religious traditions and manmade ideas?"

We want to see God as He really is, yet our experiences with people, especially those who've misrepresented Him, might have caused our vision to become distorted.

Remember how I saw God as far away and impersonal, how I believed that He wasn't really interested in me, but wanted to use me for what I could do for Him? I didn't think God would take care of me and my family. I thought it was up to me, and eventually, all good things would come to an end. I thought God was waiting for me to mess up, so He could prove me wrong and show Himself right, piously teaching me a lesson. With these beliefs, there was no way I could trust Him. No wonder I kept Him at a distance. But my beliefs about the Lord, which were based on my experiences with people and manmade rules and ideas, were wrong.

On a Saturday morning I was in my kitchen making tea and talking to God. I was voicing my complaint about one of our teenagers who was pushing limits and challenging our authority. In the midst of my complaining, I thought about my own life, about how often I chose my own comfort and ideas instead of trusting God's heart and following His way. I wondered if the Father felt the same frustration toward me that I was feeling toward my child. So, I asked Him, "How do you do it? How do you put up with me?"

Kindly and swiftly, the Father replied; His Spirit whispered, *"I have loved you with an everlasting love"* (Jer. 31:3 NIV).

God is not like the people who hurt us and let us down. His love is not limited, and His heart doesn't change based on what we do or don't do. His love is consistent and everlasting; it's a forever kind of love. We must separate our hurts, frustrations, and the ways people have let us down from the God who created us. He is the perfect Lover

> *God is not like the people who hurt us and let us down. His love is consistent and everlasting; it's a forever kind of love.*

of our soul and the only One worthy of our complete trust. God is the perfect Father, and He accepts us just as we are, while helping us form into a more beautiful creation. He has ample time for each one of us and keeps His eyes on us as though we were His only child. The Father never stops hoping the best for us, never gives up, and He never leaves. It's all about love. And the more we know Him, the more we trust Him. This trust unlocks our hearts before the Lord and enables us to experience more and more of His love and to place our lives completely in His hands.

How can we know God more, so we can trust Him in this way? We remember our need for Jesus and believe that what He has done is enough. We rest in the truth that we are saved by faith and God's grace, and we resist striving to be made right with God. We believe God is good and choose intimacy instead of distance, and close relationship over striving, every time. We remember the rules of religion are a heavy weight and how that burden never came from God. It comes from a mindset of fear and the actions of people trying to maintain control.

God is not heavy, and He never places heaviness on us. Like a falling feather, He is light and His banner over us is *love*. Receive the words of Jesus: "Come to me, all of you who are weary and carry heavy burdens, and I will give you rest. Take my yoke upon you. Let me teach you, because I am humble and gentle at heart, and you will find rest for your souls. For my yoke is easy to bear, and the burden I give you is light" (Matt. 11:28–30).

To share a deeper relationship with God and to better know His nature, we'll make His inspired words of Scripture our basis of truth. We will believe in the Bible. It won't be to prove that we're right or to manipulate desired behavior, or to earn God's favor. We'll search Scripture, simply to know Him more. Some stories of Scripture are inexplicable and unlike anything we've experienced. Some parts are confusing and even seem to contradict. Although we tend to distrust and fear what we don't understand, if we'll be willing to open God's Word with a humble heart and an open mind simply desiring to discover Him more, then we'll most certainly find Him there.

When we believe in the Bible, we're not only getting to know the Lord and learning from the historical accounts of the people who have gone before us, we're also placing our faith in the Person of God. We don't have to fully understand, we simply have to exercise our faith and choose to believe. Through His Word, God will speak to us about Himself and teach us His ways. He will show us who we are and inspire us to become more like who He created us to be. He will transform us from within by helping us believe and live out what is true. Consider this truth, "What-ever the revelation-light exposes, it will also correct, and every-thing that reveals truth is light to the soul" (Eph. 5:13 TPT). We'll discuss more of the significance of reading Scripture in chapter 8, but for now, let's choose to believe in the Bible to better know God, to open ourselves honestly before Him, and to become a living, breathing house where the Lord loves to live.

What we believe about God and ourselves is closely con-nected. In my crushing, when I found that God loved and cher-ished me, His truth finally be-came worth more than people's opinions. So, I began to pay at-tention to what He had to say about me. I started listening for His thoughts and prioritized His voice. Reading His Word and listening for His guidance, I began to hear God speak. Once He secured me as being one who was seen and loved by Him, He started to reveal what He'd created me to do.

> *What we believe about God and ourselves is closely connected.*

First of all, I was to love and worship Him, and to spend time with Him enjoying His presence. It wasn't a chore or burden-some task. It was life-giving and fulfilling. He showed me I was made to be free, filled with wonder, and childlike, and at the same time, strong and confident in Him. I began to enjoy spend-ing time with myself and the Lord, and peace started to simmer down into my soul. I could have never discovered these things on my own. It was only in close connection, in asking and listen-ing, that I was enabled to hear. I heard because I trusted Jesus enough to welcome Him to speak into my life.

What about you? What is it that you're believing about yourself? Do you believe you have value and are worth searching for? Do you believe you are loved by God and that He wants to help you discover who you really are, no matter your age? Will you believe you do hear the Shepherd's voice? Are you willing to welcome Him into shepherding and refining every part of you?

John, one of Jesus' disciples, *believed* so much that he dared to call himself *the one whom Jesus loved*. This same John wrote, "The light of God's love shined within us when he sent his matchless Son into the world so that we might live through him. This is love: He loved *us long before we loved him*. It was his love, not ours. He proved it by sending his Son to be the pleasing sacrificial offering to take away our sins" (1 John 4:9–10 TPT). God has given His all for us. He has proven His love. We are the beloved, not because we've done anything to deserve it, but because He simply loves us that much. Will we dare to be like John and believe it?

We need a shepherd and refiner, because there is an enemy actively fighting against us, whispering lies to bring deception and cause our destruction. Do we believe that the devil desires to do us harm?

When Jesus described our enemy, He proclaimed, "He was a murderer from the beginning. He has always hated the truth, because there is no truth in him. When he lies, it is consistent with his character; for he is a liar and the father of lies" (John 8:44). And in John 10:10, Jesus taught, "The thief's purpose is to steal and kill and destroy."

The demonic whispers we hear cause us to question the Lord in unbelief, because the devil seeks to steal God's glory and deceive us with a perverted twisting of the truth. He tells us that if we fully surrender our lives to the Lord, that God will humiliate us, hurt us, or force us to do something that we'd never want to do. So we hold some back, just in case the Father isn't all the way good. But that's the biggest hoax of all. Instead of being hurt by God when we believe in Him and surrender completely, we are drawn in and loved like we've never been loved before. Instead of being exposed and embarrassed, we're hidden in His forgiveness, mercy, and love. Instead of being forced into a life we don't want, we find utter joy in the things that delight His heart. He knows us better than we even know ourselves and He delights in surprising us with discoveries along the way.

When we believe, we find heaven bursting open as God speaks purpose and brings fulfillment within the dreams He shares with us. He stretches us through challenges, encouraging our growth, and provides good ground for learning while we make mistakes. All the while, He's smiling because He believes in us and knows what beauty we're becoming, even while we're still being transformed. This is the life the Lord wants for us, if we'll only believe. Our good Father can be trusted, completely, but the devil cannot.

We don't need to be afraid of the devil; we need to become comfortable with trusting in God and resting in His strength. When I think about the loving marriage I share with my husband, John, I picture what it's like to be comfortable with trusting in God. In the covenant that John and I share, there's safety and covering for me under his leadership. There's power and protection in his wise counsel and there's strength in our unity. I respect his position of authority and I trust him because I know that his heart is for me. He doesn't diminish my identity; he highlights it and encourages me as I'm growing into my best self. He celebrates my uniqueness and champions my accomplishments. When I make mistakes, he doesn't want to embarrass me by exposing, teasing, or shaming me. He waits until we're alone and pulls me in close, to speak the truth in a reassuring voice that demonstrates he wants the very best for me and the life that we share. John's belief in me makes me want to be the beauty he sees when he looks at me. It's not always perfectly played out in our marriage, yet the example demonstrates the trusting relationship that we share with the Lord.

The world might say that a wife under the authority of her husband is weak, but why would we want to be outside of this kind of loving relationship and its covering of protection, provision, and peace? This picture of a trusting marriage is God's perfect design, not only for families, but for Jesus Christ and us, His bride.

In Ephesians Paul explains, "Marriage is the beautiful design of the Almighty, a great and sacred mystery of Christ and his church. So every married man should be gracious to his wife just as he is gracious to himself. And every wife should be tenderly devoted to her husband" (Eph. 5:32–33 TPT).

The beloved, the bride of Christ, is who we are. Completely comfortable under His leadership is how we want to live. We are protected there. Our identity flourishes there. And we become all we're meant to be there as we trust the leading of our loving God.

Continuing the sifting, let's also consider the people or things we've given priority. What do we give first place in our lives? If we put our children, spouse, parents, friends, pastor or priest, or anyone in the place where God is meant to be, then we make them an idol. Let me explain. For many years in my marriage, I looked to my husband to supply what I was missing on the inside. I wasn't cognizant of my deep need to be fully known and unconditionally accepted and loved—just as I was, but I expected him to meet those needs. When John failed to supply unconditional approval and enough attention, I grew disappointed and discontent. What pressure I'd placed on the man who had promised to be my partner and the leader of our home, not my personal savior. When we had children, being a mother brought such joy and delight, but even the little ones who'd grown within my womb couldn't heal all my hurts or meet my deepest longings.

Loving my family above God and pressing them into making me whole displaced God and put an expectation on my loved ones they couldn't fulfill. No one was meant to take the Lord's place and no one can fill the desire to be seen and celebrated like the Lord. Expecting others to meet the needs only God can meet causes us disappointment. It causes resentment and frustration, leaving us unsatisfied and wanting. People, work, money, and things were never meant to fulfill the unconditional first love and contentment that only comes in relationship with God. He has a design for all things, and in our rebuilding, we want to reconstruct our priorities His way.

The Lord tells us He is jealous for us and longs to have first place in our lives. In Exodus 20, God taught His people, "You must not have any other god but me. You must not make for yourself an idol of any kind or an image of anything in the heavens or on the earth or in the sea. You must not bow down to them or worship them, for I, the Lord your God, am a jealous God who will not tolerate your affection for any other gods. I lay the sins of the parents upon their children; the entire family is affected—even children in the third and fourth generations of those who reject me. But I lavish unfailing love for a thousand generations on those who love me and obey my commands" (Exod. 20:3–6). Jesus also spoke to our priorities when He taught, "If you love your father or mother more than you love me, you are not worthy of being mine; or if you love your son or daughter more than me, you are not worthy of being mine. If you refuse to take up your cross and follow me, you are not worthy of being mine. If you cling to your life, you will lose it; but if you give up your life for me, you will find it" (Matt. 10:37–39).

Jesus said, "'You must love the Lord your God with all your heart, all your soul, and all your mind.' This is the first and greatest commandment" (Matt. 22:37–38). The Lord wants us to believe in Him, to trust Him, and to put Him first. As His devoted Bride, He wants us to choose Him first and share the bond of faithfulness, tenderness, love, and devotion. These things only come with intimacy, to those who trust and love the Lord and live according to His ways. The Lord is the only One designed to fill our need and meet our deepest longings. Believing in God and making Him our first priority is the only thing that will satisfy. Truly, we are unfulfilled without complete communion with the One who made us. He longs to be our First Love and confidence. Will we search to know Him and give Him His rightful place in our hearts and lives by believing in Him and His Word? Will we honor His lordship and allow Him to build us into His perfect design? In Psalm 127:1, David wrote, "Unless the LORD builds a house, the work of the builders is wasted. Unless the LORD protects a city, guarding it with sentries will do no good." Let's trust God to be our builder. He will not let us down.

Meditate

Is there a part of God that seems heavy to you? Have any negative circumstances with people caused you to distrust Him?

What truth do you hear the Lord speaking about Himself? Write it and declare it as He reveals Himself through His Word and His Spirit.

Do you believe that the One who created you is capable and trustworthy of meeting your deepest needs? Will you give Him the opportunity?

Prayer

Father,

Thank You for being truth that doesn't change. I want my life to be built completely on You. Help me to believe in You and Your Word.

I want to know You as my First Love. Help me untangle the lies from the truth and see Your true nature apart from manmade religion and hurtful

experiences. Reveal the false things that I'm believ-
ing about You.

    I release wrong understandings. Teach me Your
truth and show me who You are.

    You are my foundation; build my life upon You.
    In Jesus' name, amen.

Chapter Four

Confession and Repentance

But when the teachers of religious law who were
Pharisees saw him eating with tax collectors and
other sinners, they asked his disciples, "Why does he
eat with such scum?"

When Jesus heard this, he told them, "Healthy people
don't need a doctor—sick people do. I have come to
call not those who think they are righteous, but those
who know they are sinners."

—MARK 2:16–17

TO CONFESS IS SIMPLY to admit. That's what the Lord
wants; He wants us to admit that we have areas of pride,
unbelief, and pain. How can we be healed of wounds if we won't
admit they're there? How can we be well if we won't admit we're
sick? Will you acknowledge the broken places that have kept you
recycling hurtful habits? Jesus came for us, the ones who need
Him, so let's not condemn ourselves for admitting the past—the
things done to hurt us and the hurt that we have done, because
great restoration comes through humbly admitting what's true.
To clear away the broken pieces and be built upon honesty and

truth, it's time to become clean through confession and repentance, and in the next chapter, we'll be ready to choose to forgive.

When we first felt conviction and repented of our wrong, and we met our Savior in salvation, we were washed completely clean. This washing is a work that is both already done and is being done. There will be times when we need to wash a memory of our experience in living water and be refreshed in the streams of truth. We'll need to leave the old things in the water and come up renewed.

For a long time, I wandered outside of the place that held my disappointments. I was afraid to go in because I thought God didn't want me to go there. I thought He'd rather I forget the past and forge on ahead. I had heard the words of Paul used to support this thinking, "But one thing I do: forgetting what lies behind and straining forward to what lies ahead, I press on toward the goal for the prize of the upward call of God in Christ Jesus" (Phil. 3:13–14 ESV). But the context suggests a letting go of the things we've done for God and a resisting of relying on our own good works. It suggests a moving onward and upward. So that leaves me wondering, what if the onward and upward way is *through* the place of disappointment? What if we need to walk through, so we can move to that higher place?

> Blessed are those who make You their strength, for they treasure every step of the journey [to Zion]. On their way through the valley of Baca, they stop and dig wells to collect the refreshing spring water, and the early rains fill the pools. They journey from place to place, gaining strength along the way; until they meet God in Zion.
>
> —PSALM 84:5–7 THE VOICE

Let's picture in our minds a place that holds the broken things, the memories that store the pain and regret. We won't settle in or make it our home, because we're meant to walk through the past. This is a place for setting up temporary tents, for sojourning, for moving through. At the entrance is a shaded green canyon where water runs and ferns line the walls left and right. This isn't just a place of sorrow, but a productive place that holds peace. A stream is flowing center, cold and clean, leading a path all the way through. The Lord is bidding us entry, so shall we go? Let's take His hand and walk into the way of truth.

Whispers are echoed here and we listen, secured in the shadow of the One who is always near. Memories haunting our minds, lurking below the surface begin to blow in. Voices tell of expectations unmet, of falling below the mark, and of moments that linger in regret. We listen and see the faces that speak of our shame. Looking at what we've been afraid of seeing, and listening to what we haven't wanted to hear, we find it's okay to be here. It's okay to wonder why. It's okay to take that broken child within by the hand and listen and help to show them the way. Believe in the child that's still a part of you and help yourself believe.

Bidding truth to come, we admit the worst and say it all aloud. Shouts are coming from our own mouths as the truth is no longer held back. We are not alone in this canyon, the King is still here, interceding. He's seen it all and grieved every moment of pain, the hurts committed by the hands and mouths of others, and the regrets caused by our own. Go ahead and grieve. Be angry. Say what you've shoved down for far too long. And let it all go.

Evening time has come, and we find fallen trees, a place for rest. The King has much to say, so we sit down and we close our eyes and we listen. Every true word spoken and received within a pure heart lightens our load. In the morning we find we're lifted, ready to move in a higher direction. This ground beneath our feet has allowed release and given new perspective and better understanding. Confession has cleared our minds and is taking us through. We're moving on with no regret, no judgment, and no pain, only purpose.

As we leave one canyon and move to the next, we're reminded of wrongs we need to make right. Here, we'll come clean and find refreshing in the stream. Our King who stays beside us doesn't condemn or shame, but walking with His Presence causes conviction. It requires correction. The regrets we're afraid of need to come out. So, we pause, turning away from His honest gaze. His voice reassures and strengthens our resolve to reveal our rebellion and hidden desires. We don't have to carry this sin alone anymore. The Lord wants our brokenness. He has already taken it, paid for it. So, we begin to confess before our perfect King, pierced by His painfully beautiful eyes. We feel our guilt and let the burning tears fall as the betrayal pours out.

There's compassion and pain in His voice as He leads us to water, deep. He wants to wash us clean. We know we're safe, but it's not a neat and tidy scene. Crimson red runs the water because a sacrifice has already been made. It's the cost of our cleansing— the bruising, the wounding, the bleeding death of Jesus. He is *both* the Son beside the Father shining victorious in glory, and the suffering One who took our place for this very moment.

Looking into His face we cry with real sorrow that has led us to repentance. Ready to be washed, the King leads us down, down, into the cold water, rushing into every space, washing out the black settled stain. Out it flows and sin falls heavy, descending into the deep. We feel His hands lifting, pulling us up, up out of the water made clean. Sparkling in the light, we take our first breath and fill our lungs with the gift of fresh air. The King's face, the most beautiful sight to behold, is looking into our eyes, our souls, and smiling, God—sharing the very air that gives us life.

This is what love looks like, feels like. It's unexpected, but we stay to swim in the water that's come clear, because this honesty and cleansing feels so good. Purposing in our heart to never forget the cost of the cleansing, we determine to live gratefully free. Our sins have been washed away from every crooked place and we have been refreshed.

> **To Him who loved us and washed us from our sins in His own blood, and has made us kings and priests to His God and Father, to Him be glory and dominion forever and ever. Amen.**
>
> —REVELATION 1:5–6 MEV

This real work of confession and repentance is not for the weary. Sin—what we've experienced and our response, brings its own pain and shame. Through our sincere sorrow, the Lord continues His work. Allow the grief to come because this pain has purpose. Simply respond, "Purify me from my sins, and I will be clean; wash me, and I will be whiter than snow. Oh, give me back my joy again; you have broken me—now let me rejoice. Don't keep looking at my sins. Remove the stain of my guilt" (Psa.

51:7–9). As our failures surface, we simply respond by allowing them to come up, admitting our sin, and asking God for forgiveness. He is not shocked nor surprised because He's been with us all along. Thank God, His love is not based on our performance, but rather, His faithfulness. As we surrender ourselves to Jesus and open our hearts to Him, His kindness leads us to repentance that causes our hearts to change. Paul explains, "For the kind of sorrow God wants us to experience leads us away from sin and results in salvation. There's no regret for that kind of sorrow. But worldly sorrow, which lacks repentance, results in spiritual death" (2 Cor. 7:10).

> **Thank God, His love is not based on our performance, but rather, His faithfulness.**

If a specific regret resurfaces often, we might need help releasing the memory of the past. Oftentimes, church on Sunday doesn't offer adequate time and opportunity to safely speak of the things we need to confess and repent. We have to *find* opportunity, because we have all failed and caused ourselves and others pain. Begin to ask the Lord to lead you to a group, a trusted friend, or a leader whose life displays authenticity and humility—evidence of closely walking with Jesus. Ask if they would be willing to listen and pray with you for forgiveness and healing, so you can put an end to the torture of the past. At the prepared time, be open and honest, confessing to the Lord with support beside you, so you can find freedom. Ask the Lord for forgiveness and then receive it. If there's resentment toward anyone, release it. If any negative ties from the incident are still holding you captive, break the tie and release the one on the other end. James 5:16 instructs us, "Confess your sins to each other and pray for each other so that you may be healed. The earnest prayer of a righteous person has great power and produces wonderful results" (Jas. 5:16). We confess, *so that we can be healed*—expect to receive it.

To extend healing and encourage restoration to reach even further, let's consider the influence our families have made on us and the impact we, in turn, also have on others. There are some attitudes and behaviors that have been passed down which negatively impact our lives. Our family ways seem so familiar that we're often unaware of their subtle influence. But to stop perpetuating unhealthy habits, we need to become more aware. Likely modeled as behavior like gossip, judgment, criticism, fear, or pride, these negative family ways can seem totally normal. But they harm our relationships, first with the Lord and then with others, and they rob our peace. They inhibit us from becoming our best. Let's ask the Lord to bring these harmful habits to our attention, and when they're apparent, let's repent and ask the Lord to help us to change. The Holy Spirit will replace old habits with new truths—one understanding at a time. We can trust that His leading will continually take us to a more peaceful and pure way of living.

Looking again at the story of Nehemiah, the one who led Israel in rebuilding the wall and securing their city, we find a man who confessed. He asked for forgiveness not only for his sin, but also for the sin of his family. In prayer, He repented, "I confess the sins we Israelites, including myself and my father's family, have committed against you" (Neh. 1:6 NIV). And after the wall was rebuilt, he led them all to confess. "Those of Israelite descent had separated themselves from all foreigners. They stood in their places and confessed their sins and the sins of their ancestors" (Neh. 9:2 NIV). We, too, are able to confess sin on behalf of ourselves and the sins of our family that continue to influence our lives, and we can receive forgiveness and full restoration. This confession will release us, our children, and anyone we influence from carrying the sin habit any further. It will end its effects on our lives. When we hold onto the beautiful traditions from our family and let go of the hurtful habits, we will be builders of good things too. We will live a life that honors the Lord, our family and ourselves, and we will leave a better legacy.

We can rejoice in our confession and believe what the Scriptures say, "*So now the case is closed. There remains no accusing voice of condemnation against those who are joined in life-union with Jesus, the Anointed One. For the 'law' of the Spirit of life flowing through the anointing of Jesus has liberated us from the 'law' of sin and death*" (Rom. 8:1–2 TPT). Cooperating with the Lord and doing things His way invites healing and restoration into our hearts and into our relationships. Since our voice holds great power, let's obey the Lord through our repentance and "close the case." As we confess, let's believe we are washed clean. We read in Acts 11:9, "Nothing is unclean if God declares it to be clean" (TPT). Because of Jesus, the Father calls us forgiven. He calls us clean. Our new confession is "*I belong to Jesus and He has washed me clean. I am who He says I am, and sin and regret no longer have any power over me!*"

Meditation

What regret causes you sorrow and keeps coming to mind? Speak it aloud as you pray the prayer below and confess the truth before the Lord. Enter into repentance. Picture yourself being washed completely clean in the river of truth.

Note: It may be helpful to have a trustworthy friend or leader with you as you repent, confess your sin, and release the past. They can pray with you and speak life and truth over you. In time, you can also be the friend for someone else walking this sacred path.

Prayer

Father,

My sin has caused much pain, and I am truly sorry. I confess _____. Please forgive me. Thank you for the Cross, and thank You, Jesus, for taking my place. I can only come to the Father because of You.

Wash me in the water of Your forgiveness and make me clean. Your Word promises, "If we confess our sins, He is faithful and just to forgive us our sins and cleanse us from all unrighteousness" (1 John 1:9 MEV). I believe I am forgiven. The power of sinful memories no longer has a hold on me, in Jesus' name.

Holy Spirit, please continue to guide me in this process.

Lord, You have also revealed the familiar sin of ____ (pride, insecurity, bitterness, jealousy, gossip, unhealthy substitutions for peace, etc.) in my family. On behalf of myself and my mother and father's families, I confess this sin and ask for your forgiveness. Please wash my family clean and stop the effects on us now, in Jesus' name.

Thank you for Your forgiveness. I receive it. I am clean before You now! In the name of Jesus, amen.

Chapter Five

Choosing to Forgive

Since God chose you to be the holy people he loves, you must clothe yourselves with tenderhearted mercy, kindness, humility, gentleness, and patience. Make allowance for each other's faults, and forgive anyone who offends you. Remember, the Lord forgave you, so you must forgive others.

—COLOSSIANS 3:12–13

IN JOHN CHAPTER 5, there's a story about a man who'd been crippled for thirty-eight years. Being a victim for so long, his relying on others and receiving attention for his need would have woven his identity with his wound. It's likely he struggled to see himself without it. But Jesus saw the lame man as healed and knew a better story was waiting. Jesus wanted to heal him and was completely able and willing, but before He touched him, He asked the man one question: "Do you want to be healed?" (v. 6 MEV).

That's the question that Jesus is asking. Do you want the pain to go away? Are you ready to be known by something other than your wounds? Will you receive healing and be raised up into your new identity?

To be healed and whole, we'll need to let go of our right to be right. We'll need to stop withholding forgiveness and release the records of wrongs. They just keep us recalling the pain and do more damage the longer we hold on anyway. If we'll choose to let go of the evidence that keeps us connected to the source of pain, then the Lord will enable us to do the work of forgiveness. He'll stop the harmful effects that unforgiveness brings. To remove the sting and power from memories, then we'll have to release our old identities—the ones with wound and crutch and mat, and step into a new name. Our healed and complete life awaits.

Forgiveness is releasing the record, to receive healing and freedom from carrying such heavy things.

To forgive isn't to pretend the wound isn't there or that it doesn't hurt. It isn't allowing the offender to continue to step on the injury and cause more pain. It's handing over the debt that the inflictor owes. It's honoring God as judge, leaving the account with Him, and trusting that He will judge rightly. Forgiveness is releasing the record, to receive healing and freedom from carrying such heavy things.

One morning during my quiet time with the Lord, He showed me a picture of what it was like to withhold forgiveness. I saw myself pushing around a wheelbarrow piled high with books that carried the negative experiences of my life. I'd held onto them for years and would often frequent the wheelbarrow, pick up a record book, and read from its pages. Each account held painful memories. Some were confusing and frustrating, and written with names that I'd trusted. Others held my bitter responses and long list of regrets. Every line left me with sorrow. How often I'd thought of my past hurts, and yet never considered the effects of nurturing such negative experiences. Each time I set my mind on pain from the past, I grew bitter and resentful and was left feeling sorry for myself. It just solidified my perception of my identity as one who'd been wounded. The negative accounts of my history did nothing to bring further healing; they just kept me reliving the sadness of the past.

It was to my advantage to let go of the books, because holding on just kept me close to the pain. But I was so familiar and comfortable with my sadness that I struggled to even *want* to let go. For a time, I considered keeping the records, in case I needed proof of the ways I'd been hurt, evidence against the ones who had done me wrong. *What would it mean to let go?* I wondered. *What would it look like to let the ones who hurt me go free?* Doing things my way had kept the wounds from healing and left me without closure. It kept me tethered to the mat and linked to a victim identity.

I wanted to let go and be healed, but I needed help to release the past. Choosing obedience before I felt like it, I surrendered—and kept on surrendering. I asked Jesus to help me let go and forgive.

In one well-worn record book, there were accounts going far back to hurts that I held from my mom. She and I have a way of seeing things so differently. Because of our differences, a mountain of misunderstanding had grown between us. When the Lord highlighted and wanted to heal the hurt, I wondered,

How do I even begin to pray for healing? How can this moun-tain be moved when the pain seems so true? God was kind as I wrestled through the pain. He led me to begin with one simple choice. He invited me to start with one small, yet meaningful decision—to say aloud, *"I forgive."* Even before wholeheartedly meaning it or believing that healing was even possible, I chose to obey the Lord. The pain of certain memories made it hard to want or hope for better things, but I continued my small offering anyway, and nurtured it, like a fragile baby bird.

A year and a half into intentionally praying and letting go, and purposing to practice respect and honor, albeit imperfectly, something happened. The Lord gave both my mother and me significant dreams on the same night. Mine spoke of sadness and shame. Hers demonstrated how I had felt—on the outside and separated from her. We were so far apart, that, although we had love for one another, it was hard to reach through the walls we'd both erected. Our dreams gave us opportunity to talk about some things that we'd never spoken of before. The Lord helped me to carefully unwrap what I'd felt for so long. It was not easy, but we both listened. In time, we gave apologies and received them. As defenses came down, my mom reminded me of the happy girl I was as a child, the one who loved to laugh. She told me she wanted me to be me. Her kindness reached to the root and helped to bring healing to the little girl within.

Sometimes, forgiveness takes time. It takes ongoing surren-der. It takes obedience. But when we're willing to let go of the re-cords, some days one page at a time, God continues to perform a miracle. He washes the pain away and reveals more of our true identity. When we release our records of offense, we're demon-strating our answer to the question Jesus asked in John's gospel. *Yes, we want to be well!* In the work we've done together thus far in the book, we've acknowledged our pain and brokenness and confessed it honestly before the Lord. Now we are ready to be healed. We are ready to stop reading our record books. We are ready to walk into our new identity.

In my vision with the wheelbarrow, I made the decision to release the accounts. My past had happened, but it didn't have to define me or hold me victim anymore. I was ready for release, and in prayer, I asked Jesus to help me burn up the books. To-gether, we piled them up and set them ablaze and watched them burn into ashes. Unburdened by such a momentous decision, I began to stomp on the books to show that the pain had no more power over me, and the ashes rose up and danced around my feet. Free from the weight that had long held me down, the very words that caused me mourning were leading me into dancing!

This was cause for celebration and a real-life representa-tion of David's words in Psalm 30:11–12, "You have turned my mourning into joyful dancing. You have taken away my clothes of mourning and clothed me with joy, that I might sing praises to you and not be silent. O Lord my God, I will give you thanks forever!"

It might seem like two tiny insignificant words in the begin-ning. It might feel like nothing is happening, but as we continue to choose forgiveness and obey God's way, there will come a time when forgiveness shines down like a flood of light. It will fill us and work through us and move us in ways unexpected.

Forgiveness comes through the Lord's strength and His power, as we are willing to keep saying yes to His question. His light will shine in the deep places and bring release. Our part is to let it go—the anger, the frustration, the hurt and disappointment, so we can dance on top of it all! Leaving our old wounded identity behind, we are free to become healed and discover who we truly are.

Meditation

Jesus is asking you, *Do you want to be healed?* Consider His offer and all that you have to gain.

What records do you need to release to the Lord? Who do you need to forgive?

What do you hear the Lord saying about your true identity?

Prayer

Father,

Thank You for forgiving me for holding onto records of wrongs and withholding forgiveness. You have seen my pain and know my wounds. I want to be healed.

I want to do things Your way, so I choose to forgive.

I forgive _____ (insert name here, even yourself) for hurting me, and I release them. Help me to burn up the books that held these painful parts of my life as I let go.

Show me my true identity. Who am I apart from my pain? Who do You say that I am? (Listen.)

Thank You for forgiving me.

In Jesus' name.

Chapter Six

A Heart Issue

**The high and lofty one who lives in eternity, the Holy
One, says this: "I live in the high and holy place with
those whose spirits are contrite and humble. I restore
the crushed spirit of the humble and revive the
courage of those with repentant hearts."**

—Isaiah 57:15

C LOSING THIS SECTION OF restoration, let's consider
the one comprehensive purpose in our painful circumstances. Our breaking gets our attention and leads us to the
heart of the Father, when we are willing to go. He longs to forgive, heal, and restore us deep within, but our hearts have to be
willing to receive. If we choose bitterness and harden part of our
heart toward Him, we'll resist His reach. If we keep up our walls
of protection and refuse to open the doors of our hearts, He will
honor it. He will never push His way in. Yet, He allows the pain
to press us into realizing our need for Him, because *His ultimate
desire is to reach our heart.*

God's love is a good and right and true kind of love. It's not a
selfish love, like our own. It doesn't push or demand. It's a love
of freedom and gives room for choice. His is a dangerous kind of
love, because it can be rejected and end in tragedy. Yet, it's what

real love looks like. The Lord allows our mistakes, poor choices, and even our rejection of Him, while continually reaching for us and offering a better way.

Though our pressing is painful, when we surrender, the Lord uses it to soften our hearts. Becoming aware of our own need is the beginning of humility. This is when the Lord draws near and not only heals our pain, but He also restores truth to the hurting child within. Instead of shaming as a natural parent might, He looks at us with love and speaks words that bring us to life. Reaching the depth of our heart is His ultimate priority. If we'll continue to respond with openness, allowing the King of glory to come through the walls we've built, He will awaken us to new life from the inside out. Like David, we respond, "Open up, ancient gates! Open up, ancient doors, and let the King of glory enter" (Psa. 24:9).

If we know the right religious answers, but our hearts are cold and far from sharing intimacy with the Lord, then we have to question—are we ready for His return? Are we ready to see Him face to face? And consider all that we'll miss in the in-between.

Jesus told a story in Luke 18 that speaks to the attitude of the heart. In the story, two men had gone to the temple to pray. The first man stood piously with his eyes closed and imagined himself as righteous and worthy because of all the good things he had done. Strictly following the religious laws, he used his works to build himself up. He compared himself to others and inflated his own value by lowering theirs.

As the other man in the story prayed, he remained aware of his need for God. In humility, he cried out to the Lord and admitted his depravity. He didn't build himself up based on what he had done, and he didn't compare himself to anyone else. Instead, he looked at himself rightly, and saw a sinner in need of God. This was the man whom Jesus declared righteous. Jesus explained, "I tell you, this sinner, not the Pharisee, returned home justified before God. For those who exalt themselves will be humbled, and those who humble themselves will be exalted" (Luke 18:14). The man Jesus declared as righteous positioned his heart in humility and was filled with gratitude for the love of the Lord. He was the one who Jesus exalted.

As a Christian for many years, I came to see myself as justified, just like the pious man in the temple. Pride offered a fake form of significance. I bought it, and became self-righteous and judgmental, just like the ones who Jesus condemned. Francis Frangipane explains:

> A hypocrite is a person who excuses his own sin while condemning the sins of another. He is not merely "two-faced," for even the best of us must work at single-mindedness in all instances. A hypocrite, therefore, is one who refuses to admit he is, at times, two-faced, thereby pretending a righteousness that he fails to live by... Since he seeks no mercy, he has no mercy to give; since he is always under God's judgment, judging is what comes through him. (13)

Often, it's much more comfortable to focus on the problems of others than to deal with the issues of our own heart. Every one of us has been disappointed and we've all let others down. As long as we mask our brokenness and compensate by comparing ourselves to others, or focusing on the problems of someone else, then we postpone our healing. Pride wants to protect our ego and keep us from acknowledging our need. Shame even tells us to hide and to point out the sin in others. But as long as we hide from the truth within our heart, we won't be free. We must stop judging the people around us and acknowledge our own faults. Doing so allows the Lord to work in us, and eventually, through us. Are we willing to get honest with ourselves and admit we need to be completely covered in Jesus' righteousness and not our own?

Pride is an evil we'll continue to battle. If we remain afraid of exposing our pain and imperfection, then our healing, growth, and purpose will be delayed. Consider that which we fear: people really knowing us, knowing our weakness. Yet, we all have need. It's ridiculous when we look at it so plainly, but pride causes us to harden our hearts and hide from the truth. To be healed and whole, we need the remedy for pride—we need a tender and humble heart. Our depth of healing is directly related to our on-going willingness to choose humility.

Pride is a bigger problem than we may realize because God resists us when we're proud. David, a mighty king but humble man devoted to God's heart explained, "Though the Lord is great, he cares for the humble, but he keeps his distance from the proud" (Psa. 138:6). How does God feel toward us when we choose pride? Proverbs 16:5 explains, "The Lord detests all the proud of heart. Be sure of this: They will not go unpunished" (NIV). And 1 Peter 5:5 tells us, "And all of you, dress yourselves in humility as you relate to one another, for 'God opposes the proud but gives grace to the humble.'"

Pride opposes God, but humility attracts Him. Peter continues his directive in chapter 5, "So humble yourselves under the mighty power of God, and at the right time he will lift you up in honor. Give all your worries and cares to God, for he cares about you" (vv. 6-7). Note that humility is related to resisting worry and to trusting in God. Humility helps us to see ourselves accurately, to freely acknowledge our need, and to receive the merciful blessings God has for us by trusting Him in all things.

> *Humility helps us see ourselves accurately, acknowledge our need, and receive the merciful blessings God has for us.*

Francis Frangipane explains, "How can we be transformed if we do not have the capacity to see what we must change? *Humility is the spiritual faculty that enables us to perceive our need*" (5). Choosing humility, we simply admit we aren't God and we have need of the One who is. We repent for attempting to take His place and we welcome Jesus to be LORD over every part of our lives. We welcome Him to be the Center of it all, responding like David did, "Lead me to the rock that is higher than I" (Psa. 61:2).

Humility keeps us mindful of the gift of salvation we've been given and helps us to rightly see ourselves as totally reliant on the Lord. It helps us live with appreciation and trust for our King. Choosing humility deflates the pride of self, and instead, gives glory to God. It attracts His Presence. It sets us free from the bondage of perfection and striving and helps us rest in the Lord—in all that *He* has done, is doing, and will do. Humility shakes us free from others' expectations and allows us to believe that we are accepted, just as we are. It helps us hope for continual renewal and postures us to receive from the Lord.

Zephaniah 3:12 says, "Those who are left will be the lowly and humble, for it is they who trust in the name of the Lord." We are the ones who are left; we have survived the shaking and our breaking has led us to open our hearts before the Lord. Looking for Him with undivided hearts, we are finding Him. We are finding a close God who deeply cares for us. Seeing Him as He really is, we know the One our hearts adore. We trust Him and open the door of our lives completely, crying, "I found the one I adore! I caught him and fastened myself to him, *refusing to be feeble in my heart again.* Now I'll bring him back to the temple within where I was given new birth—into my innermost parts, the place of my conceiving" (SOS. 3:4 TPT).

Let's continue to allow the Holy Spirit to till the soil of our hearts, breaking up the hardened ground and bringing to light the broken places so the Lord can continue His work. We simply respond sincerely, "Create in me a clean heart, O God. Renew a loyal spirit within me. Do not banish me from your presence, and don't take your Holy Spirit from me. Restore to me the joy of your salvation, and make me willing to obey you" (Psa. 51:10–12). Let's fully welcome Jesus and give Him room. He will neither overwhelm us nor rush this process. He has all the time we need, and He is always available. Our Father God is always near, and every time we humble our hearts before Him, we find

Him, present and attentive. The more we get to know Him, the more we believe and trust Him, and that is all He asks. He will do the rest.

> Now, this is what Yahweh says: "*Listen*, Jacob, to the One who created you, Israel, to the one who shaped who you are. Do not fear, for I, your Kinsman-Redeemer, will rescue you. I have called you by name, and you are mine. When you pass through the deep, *stormy* sea, you can count on me to be there with you. When you pass through *raging* rivers, You will not drown. When you walk through *persecution* like fiery flames, you will not be burned; the flames will not harm you, for I am your Savior, Yahweh, your mighty God, the Holy One of Israel!"
>
> —ISAIAH 43:1–3 TPT

Meditation

What is the current condition of your heart? Is there any pride hiding within? Will you invite Jesus to be present in every part?

Prayer

Father,
Thank You for being a safe place for my heart. You're a good Father, better than the best example on this Earth. Thank You for never giving up on me and for faithfully pursuing me. I trust the truth of 1 Peter 2:6: "As the Scriptures say, 'I am placing a cornerstone in Jerusalem, chosen for great honor, and anyone who trusts in him will never be disgraced.'"
I repent of fear, pride, and distrust, and I open

my heart completely to You. You know everything about me and love me just the same. Help me to choose humility and to keep my heart open and pliable before You.

Though I struggle with pride, fear, doubt, ____, You call me forgiven. I am washed clean because of Your sacrifice, Jesus. Your Spirit lives within me and enables me to live beyond my own limitations. In You, I am alive, and I am free! Shape me into Your beautiful design.

Thank You for loving me so well.

I love You too.

SECTION 2:

THE LOAF OF BREAD
—Our Sustenance—

**The God of heaven, He will enable us to prosper.
Therefore we His servants will arise and build....**

—Nehemiah 2:20 mev

W E HAVE FULLY OPENED and surrendered our hearts
to Jesus and given Him His rightful place as Lord. He
has done a deep work within, and now we need the ongoing sustenance that He gives, to nourish and sustain us. With our appreciation and wholehearted devotion, we're ready to have our
lives built on Jesus Himself. Although the Lord is the One who
does the work, we have a part to play. We must keep our hearts
soft and open before the Lord and continue to choose humility. Responding with trust and obedience to each revelation and
truth that God gives is another piece of our part.

We must continue to seek Christ as our First Love and learn
to love Him with all of our hearts, souls, and minds. No longer
after Him for what He can do for us, now we seek Him for who
He is. Consider this verse that demonstrates the importance of

our motive, "Now when he was in Jerusalem at the Passover Feast, many believed in his name when they saw the signs that he was doing. But Jesus on his part did not entrust himself to them, because he knew all people and needed no one to bear witness about man, for he himself knew what was in man" (John 2:23–25 ESV).

We want Jesus to entrust Himself to us. So, in this ongoing journey of life and relationship, we'll need to partake in all that the Lord provides for the road ahead. We'll need every life-giving element that is necessary for becoming a trustworthy dwelling place. It will take time to learn and practice this daily partaking of the Lord, but we can trust God's timing and remember that He gives grace to be the new creation that honors and houses His Presence. Jesus said, "The bread of God is the One who came out of heaven to give his life to feed the world. … I am the Bread of Life. Come every day to me and you will never be hungry. Believe in me and you will never be thirsty" (John 6:33, 35 TPT).

Let's give our full commitment and dedication to discovering, receiving, and absorbing the necessary sustenance that Jesus gives, so we can learn His ways and grow up in Him. Let's unlock the mysteries of obedience, freedom, and becoming our truest selves. Let's partake of the pleasures found in the nourishment of Jesus, for He sustains us with all we need until the very end.

Chapter Seven

Seeking to Know All of God

"Go, inspect the city of Jerusalem. Walk around and
count the many towers. Take note of the fortified
walls, and tour all the citadels, that you may describe
them to future generations. For that is what God is
like. He is our God forever and ever, and he will guide
us until we die."

—PSALM 48:12–14

THERE ARE SO MANY mysteries in God! Perhaps the
greatest of them all is that this visionary Creator of everything desires to be in close relationship with you and me! We
may forever be uncovering the beautiful facets and truths about
Him. And He is a treasure well worth our seeking! Let's look
together to discover more of God and His character, as He is
fully expressed in three persons—the Father, Jesus the Son, and
the Holy Spirit. Every person of the Godhead is vital and each
One has specific contributions to make in our lives. May this in-
troduction make us hungry to pursue, welcome, and enjoy each
part of Him more.

In Jeremiah 29:13–14 God said, "'If you look for me whole-heartedly, you will find me. I will be found by you,' says the Lord. 'I will end your captivity and restore your fortunes. I will gather you out of the nations where I sent you and will bring you home again to your own land.'"

To give us an image of His strength and security, the Lord showed me a picture of a wall surrounding a kingdom. Remember the children's story of *Jack and the Beanstalk*? If the giant had a wall surrounding his home, it wouldn't even compare to the massive structure I saw. This barrier was the widest, tallest, and strongest stone wall. Homes were built inside of this wall with people living within; it was a fortress within itself. Can you envision living in this safe land where joyful memories are made and the perfect love of the Lord resides?

God wants us to know Him as that protection. Because we love and trust in Him, we get to live within Him. Psalm 48:3 explains, "God himself is in Jerusalem's towers, revealing himself as its defender." He is our strong foundation and the wall of peace surrounding our hearts and minds. When troubles come, we may feel the wind and we may sense the rain on our skin, but the storm will not take us out because Jesus Christ is our Lord and fortress. God is our true *home*.

To secure ourselves within this wall, we'll need to seek the very Person of wisdom—Christ the Creator. His wisdom is different from that of the world, and in order to receive and experience His understanding, we'll need to humbly let go of our own ideas and search for His, like treasures to be found. Let's seek, together now, and discover how our lives can be built upon the wisdom of Christ so that we can be a dwelling place for Him.

Not only do we get to enjoy the security of abiding in God, we also want to be a place where He loves to reside. In the book of John chapter 2, we read about how the many people who saw Jesus perform miracles quickly believed. Let's look at Jesus' response, "Now while he was in Jerusalem at the Passover Festival, many people saw the signs he was performing and believed in his name. But Jesus would not entrust himself to them, for he knew all people. He did not need any testimony about mankind, for he knew what was in each person" (23-25 NIV). How can we reach beyond our own self-serving ways and become a life the Lord entrusts Himself to?

Jesus taught us as He prayed, "And this is the way to have eternal life—to know you, the only true God, and Jesus Christ, the one you sent to earth" (John 17:3). To seek and know God more, let's begin by focusing on Jesus—God's Son and the Father's expression of Himself upon the earth. Scripture says, "The Son is the dazzling radiance of God's splendor, the exact expression of God's true nature—his mirror image!" (Heb. 1:3 TPT).

Jesus shows us what God is like. And He also looks like us! He walked where we walk and experienced the same joys, disappointments, temptations, and sufferings we do. Yet, He did it all just right! Hebrews 4:15-16 explains, "For we do not have a high priest who is unable to empathize with our weaknesses, but we have one who has been tempted in every way, just as we are—yet he did not sin. Let us then approach God's throne of grace with confidence, so that we may receive mercy and find grace to help us in our time of need" (NIV). Jesus is the example that we look to and model our own lives after. Over and over again, He demonstrated a life of love, service, and sacrifice. He showed us how perfect love and uncompromised truth can coexist. His was a life worthy of trust.

Because we believe in Jesus, our right-standing with God has been restored! Receiving our healing, renewing our mind, and learning to think and act like Jesus is an ongoing process, but the ability to go before the Father is forever finished. Jesus' righteousness opens the door for us to be welcomed into the family of God!

> *Receiving our healing, renewing our mind, and learning to think and act like Jesus is an ongoing process.*

Because of Him, we can face the Father truly guiltless and completely brand new. Apart from Him, there's no way to this new life or to intimacy with God. But with Jesus, we're washed clean and know the way to come in close! Paul explained, "But now in Christ Jesus you who once were far away have been brought near by the blood of Christ" (Eph. 2:13 NIV).

After entering humanity and finishing the work He came to do, Jesus returned to be with the Father in heaven. There, He reigns victorious, ministering and interceding for us (see Romans 8:34). But before He left, Jesus explained how He made the way for us to know the Father-heart of God. Jesus said, "I am the way, the truth, and the life. No one can come to the Father except *through me*" (John 14:6, my emphasis). It's such a familiar passage that we might overlook the depth of what Jesus was saying. But we don't want to miss this.

Like a passage door, Jesus makes God accessible. He is the way for us to enter into a restored relationship with the Father as a beloved daughter or son. Jesus has shown us the Father—His purity, compassion, authority, and faithfulness. He's shown us the great extent of the Father's love. So let's not stop at the door, let's go in and fellowship with our Father. Let's draw

> *The ability to go before the Father is forever finished. Jesus' righteousness opens the door for us to be welcomed into the family of God!*

close to the very One who imagined and designed us in detail. He drafted remarkable plans for our lives and inscribed them in a special book. We can read all about it in Psalm 139. That's where our Abba Father assures us that He knows us and remembers what He's placed inside.

He's a good Father who's into the details and longs to make known His love and dreams for us. He wants to help us become all that He's imagined us to be and enable us to carry out His good plans. Just like a loving Dad, we can rely on Him while growing to be like Him and maturing into His likeness. He has a rich inheritance for us and longs to train us in caring for and extending His Kingdom. Like the father in the story of a dad's extravagant love told in Luke 15, our Father is always watching the road, always hoping and believing for the best, while whispering His wisdom and calling us closer. Whenever we listen, we will *always* hear love in His voice.

We have great need of this Father, and He's ready to give us His love, insight, correction, and wisdom. Sometimes, though, we have trouble receiving from Him because our thinking is limited to what we know. Some of our experiences with our earthly father or people who represented the Lord have negatively tainted our view of Father God.

I remember thinking it sounded strange when people prayed to God and called Him "*Father*." It seemed so intimate, so assuming. I was familiar with Jesus, felt His love for me, but I wasn't sure about the Father. It seemed better to stick close to Jesus and let Him speak to the Father on my behalf. And Jesus does that for me, and for you, but He also wants us to know our Creator Dad for ourselves.

Paul helps us better understand, "And because we are his children, God has sent the Spirit of his Son into our hearts, prompting us to call out, 'Abba, Father.' Now you are no longer a slave but God's own child. And since you are his child, God has made you his heir" (Gal. 4:6–7).

Another book that helped me better grasp the love of the Father was *Experiencing Father's Embrace*. In it, Jack Frost explained:

> Religion has misrepresented the nature of Father God and portrayed Him to be something He is not. The idea that Father is the vengeful arm of the Trinity and that Jesus is the compassionate One pleading for our undeserved pardon, is not just harmful to our relationship with God, but it runs totally contrary to the teaching of Jesus. Jesus came to demonstrate who the Father is and what He is like, and He does

this through His words and actions. To gain a true picture of Father's feelings toward His children, it is best to turn to the One whose purpose it was to show us the Father. (59)

Jesus has shown us the Father's perfect love. It's unconditional, different from the love we have known and shown. In fact, it's so good it can be hard to believe that it's really true.

When we believe God's love can't be that good, we might think we need to earn it. Deep down, we might even fear that if we're not careful, it'll be taken away. But that's not the case. The Father always loves us just as we are. Jack Frost taught, "There is nothing you can do to cause God to love you any more than He does right now. There is nothing you can do to cause God to love you any less than He does right now. Unconditional love is never based upon the merit of the one receiving it; it is based upon the loving nature of the one giving it" (64).

We desperately need the Father to enlighten us about His perfect love, in order to perceive and receive Him as He really is.

To grow in relationship with the Father, we can seek to know how Jesus related to Him while He was on the earth. He often withdrew from others to spend time alone with His Dad (see Luke 5:16). Jesus honored and trusted His Father so much that He often sought His input (see John 5:19). And He lived boldly because He stayed connected to His Dad's acceptance, wisdom, and love. That's how the Father wants us to live too, asking and listening for what He has to say, and trusting Him so much that we believe and live by His every word.

At times, we'll hear Him correct us, because that's what good fathers do. As a good Father, He loves us enough to give us free choice and allow us to learn through experiencing challenges *with Him*. He isn't afraid of our mistakes, no. In fact, He often uses them to bring us closer and to redirect and refine us. We can know that He will never trick us or cause us pain to teach us a lesson. That's neither the Father's heart nor His way. He is always working things out for our good. As Psalm 145:8–9 says, "The Lord is merciful and compassionate, slow to get angry and filled with unfailing love. The Lord is good to everyone. He showers compassion on all his creation."

Our Father loves us so much that He continually provides just what we need. He began with the Law, to show His people a safe and right way to live so they could be near Him—a holy God. And when the Law proved we all needed a Savior, the Father provided that too, by giving a part of Himself, His own Son. Paul, a former devoted keeper of the Law who was changed by experiencing the truth and love of the Lord explains:

> The law of Moses was unable to save us because of the weakness of our sinful nature. So God did what the law could not do. He sent his own Son in a body like the bodies we sinners have. And in that body God declared an end to sin's control over us by giving his Son as a sacrifice for our sins. He did this so that the just requirement of the law would be fully satisfied for us, who no longer follow our sinful nature but instead follow the Spirit.
>
> —ROMANS 8:3–4

Father God is the best Father, and He's given us Jesus so we can walk through the door and climb onto His lap as His beloved child. He's ready for us to join Him at the family table and experience His lavishing love and the blessing of being His heir. He's the Father that death can't take away and the One who never disappoints or abandons. He loves us without conditions, and He remains faithful until the very end.

This same God who is perfect love is also holy and just. We can't look at one truth without the other. God is not like us; His perspective and understanding are much greater than ours. Song of Songs 5:12 says, "He sees everything with pure understanding. How beautiful his insights—without distortion. His eyes rest upon the fullness of the river of revelation, flowing so clean and pure" (TPT). His ways truly are higher than ours. God explains, "'For my thoughts are not your thoughts, neither are your ways my ways,' declares the Lord. 'As the heavens are higher than the earth, so are my ways higher than your ways and my thoughts than your thoughts'" (Isa. 55:8–9 NIV). He is a just God who hates sin, because He sees what it breeds and produces.

In Isaiah chapter 6, the author and prophet tells about a vision where he "clearly saw the Lord." He recorded, "He was seated on his exalted throne, towering high above me. His long, flowing robe of splendor spread throughout the temple" (vv. 1-2 TPT). And he tells of the creatures around the throne that cried, "Holy, holy, holy is the Lord God, Commander of Angel Armies! The whole earth is filled with his glory!" (v. 3). Isaiah's response was telling. He cried, "Woe is me! I'm destroyed—doomed as a sinful man! For my words are tainted and I live among people who talk the same way" (v. 5). When we rightly see God our response is similar to Isaiah's. We're awakened to His holiness.

This is why we appreciate the righteousness of Jesus. Only because of Him can we have clean hands and pure hearts and share a close relationship with our loving and righteous Father (Psa. 24:3–5). Through Jesus, God has made a new covenant with us: "But this is the new covenant I will make with the people of Israel on that day, says the Lord: I will put my laws in their minds, and I will write them on their hearts. I will be their God, and they will be my people" (Heb. 8:10). The blood of Jesus enables us to come close to this holy God by giving us a new heart and the promise of enabling us to obey.

But we need to know, how do we continue to believe and learn to live as God's trustworthy child? How do we live out this precious gift of new covenant and new life? It's only possible with the confirmation and help of the Holy Spirit. Only with the Spirit of God Himself resting on us—filling, empowering, and leading us can we go on to live a holy life that honors our King!

Who, then, is this mysterious part of God called the Holy Spirit? Who is the One who rested on Jesus as a dove (Luke 3:21–22) and was promised to His followers? (John 14:15–21). We find Him in the very first book and chapter of our Bibles when we read, "In the beginning God created the heavens and the earth. The earth was formless and empty, and darkness covered the deep waters. And the Spirit of God was hovering over the surface of the waters" (Gen. 1:1-3).

Like Jesus, the Spirit of God was with God and a part of God from the very beginning. He was there at creation, empowering life's potential and watching it burst forth. He was there, hovering with wonder as breath formed words and creation was born! He was there contributing when particles gathered at the Father's command. He was there when massive waves of water and whitecaps rushed the surface of the earth in full wonder explosion as the Father's voice thundered out, "*Let the waters beneath the sky flow together into one place*" (Gen. 1:9).

Imagine the three—Father, Son, and Spirit, unified in contribution and celebration. The Spirit of God was there, and He is here, still participating in the creation of new things, given to abide with all who believe. He is the One who makes new things possible! (See Romans 8:5–11.)

To become a dwelling place that the Lord Jesus does entrust Himself to, God has given us the Holy Spirit. He enables us to know God and become the new creation that the Father designed us to be! Jesus said, "I will ask the Father, and He will give you another Helper, who will stay with you forever. He is the Spirit, who reveals the truth about God" (John 14:16–17 GNT). Jesus and the Father have given the most generous gift, and according to Acts 2:39–40, He is for *all* who believe. "Peter replied, 'Each of you must repent of your sins and turn to God, and be baptized in the name of Jesus Christ for the forgiveness of your sins. Then you will receive the gift of the Holy Spirit. This promise is to you, and to your children, and to those far away—*all* who have been called by the Lord our God.'" A representative of the Godhead, the Holy Spirit comes to us with salvation and confirms that we have been reborn as a child of God. He enables us to really believe we are loved, forgiven, and fully accepted. Receive this truth: "And you did not receive the 'spirit of religious duty,' leading you back into the fear of never being good enough. But you have received the 'Spirit of full acceptance,' enfolding you into the family of God. And you will never feel orphaned, for as he rises up within us, our spirits join him in saying the words of tender affection, 'Beloved Father!' For the Holy Spirit makes God's fatherhood real to us as he whispers into our innermost being, 'You are God's beloved child!'" (Rom. 8:15–16 TPT).

Although Scripture speaks of this gift from God, some still have reservations. Some churches teach that the things of the Holy Spirit are no longer for today. Others encourage emotional reactions and call it all the work of the Holy Spirit. Both extremes can cause us to question and leave us wondering who He is and how He fits into our lives.

We need to know, because when the Holy Spirit is misunderstood our tendency can be to push Him aside. That was my experience. I thought of Him as a force that would blow in and cause people to act out emotionally. I sensed the power of His Presence and was unsure of what I didn't understand. There were times when I resisted Him, trying to keep control, and times when I worked up my own emotional response, attempting to force His hand. Instead of honestly seeking to know the Holy Spirit as a Person of God, I kept Him at a distance.

Not long before my dad died, we sat together in his hospital room talking about the Holy Spirit. I explained my confusion and Dad suggested I read *Good Morning Holy Spirit*, by Benny Hinn. I found that as I genuinely sought the Holy Spirit as a unique part of God, my fear lessened, and I realized that

He wasn't pushy. Yes, He was powerful, but He was also gentle, careful, and considerate. Like a link, He enabled me to *know* the Father and the Son. In his book, Hinn explained, "The Holy Spirit is a person. And just like you, He can feel, perceive, and respond. He gets hurt. He has the ability to love and the ability to hate. He speaks, and He has His own will. But exactly who is He? The Holy Spirit is the Spirit of God the Father and the Spirit of God the Son. He is the power of the Godhead—the power of the Trinity" (48). If we choose to resist this gentle, yet mighty Spirit of God, He will respect our choice. But we will miss the peace, power, and purpose that He brings to our lives and we won't experience the fullness of knowing God. If we choose to leave the Holy Spirit out of our daily lives and quiet His whisper, and if we shun Him from our gatherings with other believers, we are rejecting the sacred gift from Jesus and the Father.

Like any gift that is given, the Holy Spirit can either be set aside and ignored—like I had done for years—or be appreciated and enjoyed. To appreciate the Holy Spirit is to believe in the gift, to welcome Him into our daily lives, and to honor Him as a valuable contributing part of God. I can now attest that as we get to know the Holy Spirit, we find Him trustworthy and the One who works with us to fulfill the love and the work God has called us to share in and to do.

We need to consider why the adversary works so hard to confuse our understanding of this part of the Lord. He knows that the Holy Spirit is the source of power we need to successfully live out what we say we believe. Do we really think we can live out our new life and multiply the kingdom without this most valuable gift? Jesus and the Father gave us what they knew we would need. Once again, God has provided exactly what His children would require to know and walk with Him.

The Holy Spirit has no desire to take us over, but He does want to work with us. He wants to empower us in His strength to live aware, connected, and filled with the Lord.

The Lord wants us to receive and experience all the gifts and benefits of a life completely united with Him. He has great plans for us to grow into His original design. To satisfy our deepest hunger and become all we were created to be, and to take part in His kingdom on the earth, we must seek to know *all of God*.

Remember that God is not religion. Religion actually binds and hinders the freedom of the Lord. We won't allow the adversary to fool us into entering that confining box, because Christ broke it open two thousand years ago! It is for freedom that Jesus has set us free! Let this go deep within: "Let me be clear, the Anointed One has set us free—not partially, but completely and wonderfully free! We must always cherish this truth and stubbornly refuse to go back into the bondage of our past" (Gal. 5:1 TPT). He has no desire to chain us down or hold us back. But He does long for us to really know and share communion with Him so we can experience His freedom. He longs for us to mature and grow from that safe, wide-open space.

God the Father, Jesus the Son, and the Holy Spirit are each uniquely individual. Yet, together, they make up the One unfathomable and absolute God. What a beautiful mystery to pursue!

As we seek out relationship with each and every part of Him, we'll receive a full experience of truly knowing God. Our lives will be trustworthy, ignited for the Lord, and empowered to extend His Kingdom throughout the earth! Jesus is both the sacrificed Lamb and the victorious King who is returning one day. We must be alert and prepared! So, let's pursue and welcome every part of the Father, Son, and Spirit with great fervor even now.

Meditate

Are you resisting any part of God? Would you like to know the Father, Jesus, or the Holy Spirit better? Talk to Him about it and seek to know that Person of God through Scripture and conversation in prayer.

Prayer

Father,

I come to You in the name and righteousness of Jesus Christ. Thank You for making a way for me to be right with You. Thank You, Jesus, for being the door to the Father and for showing me what love looks like. Thank You for laying Your life down for me and taking my punishment. You've made a way for my sins to be washed away, so I can come close. I am so grateful.

Abba, deepen my understanding of who You are as my Father. I have need for You in my life. Help me to know You more as my trustworthy Life-giver and Dad.

I take off any filters of religion or preconceived ideas. (If needed) I forgive _____ for causing confusion about who You are. I open my heart to seeking and knowing all of You, for myself.

Holy Spirit, I need You and welcome You into my life. Thank You for always being with me. I want to become more aware of You and hear and trust Your voice. When I open the Scriptures, please give me revelation. Reveal more of Jesus and teach me how to be like Him. Show me the Father and help me to know Him more. Empower me to live as the new creation that I am!

Thank You, Father. Thank You, Jesus. Thank You, Holy Spirit.

I love You! I love You! I love You!
Amen.

Chapter Eight

Feed on the Word

In the same way that nursing infants cry for milk, you must intensely crave the pure spiritual milk of *God's Word*. For this "milk" will cause you to grow into maturity, fully nourished and strong for life.

—1 Peter 2:2 tpt

To know God more and to discover how He thinks and feels about us, and to be empowered to live a life worthy of His love, we can read and feed on His Word. It's so much more than fulfilling a requirement, it's getting to know the person of God and being led by His perspective.

I remember diligently reading through the Bible years ago when my dad was sick. I was desperate to do the right thing to earn God's favor. What was meant to take a year took me three, and my dad was gone by the time I'd finished. In my reading, rather than seeking to know God in relation to His Word, I worked to be accepted and to get my prayers answered. I failed to purposefully include the Lord, so without welcoming His presence I was just fulfilling an obligation. (No one wants to be pursued that way!) I was left wanting, because something was missing and that something was a real relationship.

More than just working for what He can do for me, I've learned the value of communing with God in Scripture. So, I include Him in the reading, and I ask Him for understanding. I listen for His voice and expect Him to provide the truth I need. And I always find Him there, within the pages of Scripture—bringing truth to life and feeding my soul. To know the Lord in this way, to receive His wisdom and grow in maturity, and to receive healing and light, let's set our focus on the delights of feeding on His Word!

We need help with gaining fresh perspective and building new habits. We need the Lord to provide new ways of thinking and living—daily.

> *Opening God's Word and listening for Him is like inviting Jesus to come over to visit for a while.*

Opening God's Word and listening for Him is like inviting Jesus to come over to sit around the table and visit for a while. This time with the Lord and His Word is the means to knowing our God. This is the way we get to hear what the One who loves us most sounds like. It's how we learn to recognize and trust His voice. In John 10:2–5 Jesus explains, "The one who enters by the gate is the shepherd of the sheep. The gatekeeper opens the gate for him, and the sheep listen to his voice. He calls his own sheep by name and leads them out. When he has brought out all his own, he goes on ahead of them, and his sheep follow him because they know his voice. But they will never follow a stranger; in fact, they will run away from him because they do not recognize a stranger's voice" (NIV).

When we open Scripture and ask the Lord to speak, we're joining Him at the table, listening and welcoming His influence on our lives. We're making His voice a priority. In response to our seeking, the Lord always shows up and shows us His heart—His generosity, kindness, and mercy, and the faithfulness He has toward our covenant relationship. Scripture shows us how He thinks, how He loves, and this ongoing revelation helps us love Him more in return. As our thinking shifts from seeing Scripture reading as a heavy, burdensome task to simply spending time listening to the Lord's voice and encountering our Creator, we'll find the Bible to be compelling, relevant, and the precise provision we need.

When we come hungry and ready to receive from God's Word, we'll also gain wisdom and grow in maturity, just like Jesus did (see Luke 2:52). The Word of the Lord washes the ways of the world from our thinking and resets it to truth. Breathing the truth of Scripture to life, the Holy Spirit transforms us through the living, breathing Word. Hebrews 4:12 says, "For the word of God is alive and powerful. It is sharper than the sharpest two-edged sword, cutting between soul and spirit, between joint and marrow. It exposes our innermost thoughts and desires."

Although written by mere mortal men, the words contained in the Bible originated in God's heart. Paul explained, "All Scripture is inspired by God and is useful to teach us what is true and to make us realize what is wrong in our lives. It corrects us when we are wrong and teaches us to do what is right. God uses it to prepare and equip his people to do every good work" (2 Tim. 3:16–17). When we appreciate and utilize this written gift from God, we will know the way that we should go. Following the direction given by the Lord in Scripture will redirect the course of our lives so that we walk in wisdom and fulfill the plans the Father has for us!

One such example is found in the telling of this book. Through the Book of Nehemiah, the Lord revealed the fearful way that I'd been living. And He used His Word to settle me, to heal me, and to teach me how to come out of agreement with the enemy's lies and into agreement with His protection over me. It's an ongoing process that I choose to participate in daily. He's used many Biblical truths to bring about my transformation, but a few of my favorites that have deeply impacted my life include Ezekiel 36:26–27, Matthew 5:3, and Matthew 5:14–16 (particularly in THE MESSAGE). When we allow God's Word to permeate truth into our lives, we can't help but be changed for the better!

In our seeking within the Word, there will be times when the Lord speaks correction. To me, it often feels embarrassing at first, as I realize the unbecoming ways that I've behaved. Then I ask the Holy Spirit to help me understand why and to trace it back to where it began. That's when I see where love is lacking and how I've responded to a hurt or misunderstanding. Remember how we read in the first section that the enemy deposits lies in our unhealed places? We hear the subtle voice of the enemy (which can sound like our own idea) and agree. Then there's an open door for demonic influence and darkness readily supplies ideas to bring about destruction. When the Lord reveals our sinful reactions, it's pretty hard to see, and we can sure relate with Paul in Romans 7:17–20 (TPT):

> **And now I realize that it is no longer my true self doing it, but the unwelcome intruder of sin in my humanity. For I know that nothing good lives within the flesh of my fallen humanity. The longings to do what is right are within me, but willpower is not enough to accomplish it. My lofty desires to do what is good are dashed when I do the things I want to avoid. So if my behavior contradicts my desires to do good, I must conclude that it's not my true identity doing it, but the unwelcome intruder of sin *hindering me from being who I really am.***

This is why we need the voice of the Lord continually speaking through His Word, telling us the truth. The Word of God helps us recognize and reject the lies of the enemy. We need to be willing to hear and receive the correction the Lord gives. What He wants is our honesty, openness, and surrender to His process of healing our hearts and renewing our minds. If we'll choose humility as we're learning to trust God, we'll realize that He will never embarrass us. In safe settings, He reveals the truth in His Word and exposes the areas in us that are lacking His influence. It might redden our cheeks for the moment, but we want the truth to be told so we can become healed and whole. We also want the truth so we can extend healing instead of hurt. The Lord offers us many of these good trades—our reactive defenses of fear, anger, and offense, for trust, forgiveness and empathy. As we release our pain and accompanying lies, we encounter healing revelation within the Word and voice of God, and we are supernaturally changed. The dead layers that have covered up our true selves are removed because truth is taking its place and our new, more beautiful self has room to rise! Jesus is giving life and beauty where death and ashes once resided and through this sanctification process, our lives are being made whole.

Although correction can feel sharp, the Holy Spirit confirms that the Father's rebuke is for our good. Trusting our loving Father, let's let the light of Proverbs 3:12 shine in as we yield to our transformation, "For the Lord corrects those he loves, just as a father corrects a child in whom he delights." He loves us too much to allow us stay covered up by the rubble of the world and the messes we've made. We really are children of God and in our Father's kindness, He loves us enough to rebuke, remind, and redirect us back onto the path that leads to life. Feeding on Scripture is one of the main ways we discover how to walk into our new life. It's God's correction that guides our way and keeps our paths straight, so we can continue becoming His design!

> *As we release our pain and accompanying lies, we encounter healing revelation within the Word and voice of God, and we are supernaturally changed.*

Not only do we get to experience and enjoy our own restoration, but we're also being equipped to turn to those beside us and share what we've been given. Because of our experiences, we've felt the sting of dying that sin brings. But through our healing, we also know resurrection! Equipped by traveling *through* the fire, we can bring healing and restoration with deep empathy to others who are feeling the pain of where we've once been. Let's believe, with hope and expectation, the promises of comfort that Paul describes in 2 Corinthians 1:4: "He comforts us in all our troubles so that we can comfort others. When they are troubled, we will be able to give them the same comfort God has given us."

Every time we choose to feed on God's Word we simultaneously receive what we currently need and build up a firewall of protection against the enemy. The adversary would rather we believed his lies, kept making our own way, and stayed covered up, bound to old things. But with each truth read, we're strengthened for battle against old identities of worry, doubt, pride, fear, shame, and the list goes on. Cooperating with transformation, no matter what we walk through, the Father's plans and purposes will be accomplished because we're seeking Him, listening for our Shepherd's voice, and following His lead.

The Word of God is one of the primary ways the Father speaks with His children. His words help us grow into strong, confident sons and daughters. As we stay faithful to read, meditate, and receive the Word of God, we'll discover that we're getting to know the Father, the Son, and the Holy Spirit in a deeper way. God's truth is changing the way we see and think about the Lord, ourselves, and others. Like moving from milk to solid food, we're transforming from stage to stage, in maturity and growth. We're gaining endurance and strength. Staying faithful—even in the times of waiting—and continuing to seek, we'll find that it's in this place that our faith is taking root and growing strong. Let's press into the following Scripture, asking for the Father's insight and expectant to receive every one of these rich promises:

> **Cry out for insight, and ask for understanding. Search for them as you would for silver; seek them like hidden treasures. Then you will understand what it means to fear the Lord, and you will gain knowledge of God. For the Lord grants wisdom! From his mouth come knowledge and understanding. He grants a treasure of common sense to the honest. He is a shield to those who walk with integrity. He guards the paths of the just and protects those who are faithful to him. Then you will understand what is right, just, and fair, and you will find the right way to go.**
>
> —PROVERBS 2:3–9

Practically speaking, to meet with the Lord in His Word, you may wonder where to start. Jesus asked His Father for *daily* bread. When we ask, He will always come, bringing nourishing truth. Using a daily reading plan gives a roadmap and allows the opportunity to celebrate our progress along the way. Listening for the Lord's leading, if the Holy Spirit guides you to read outside of the plan to study a specific topic or to read a certain book of the Bible, feel free to follow. The plan isn't meant to bind, but to be a guide, and God's Spirit knows just what you need.

Choosing a Bible is important, because you want to enjoy and comprehend what you're reading. Look for a version or translation that's best suited for you. My friend and mentor Margi likes to read a different Bible each year, so that's another option! With a favored Bible and journal in hand, find a comfortable place to meet with the Lord and come with faith, expectant to receive.

Acknowledge the Spirit of God and welcome Him. Then begin to read and search to see what the Holy Spirit is highlighting. Engaging your mind, be attentive to the lessons learned. Engaging your spirit, be open to correction and direction. And engaging your imagination, allow the Lord to give you fresh revelation in what you're reading. Partaking of this daily bread will give you the wisdom you need to victoriously meet the day.

As God speaks through His Word, our response is imperative. We can act on our belief and demonstrate our hope in what God has spoken. Responding to Scripture through journaling will allow the truth of God's Word to impact our lives in a greater way. As you read, look for the verses that are standing out and seem to be speaking directly to you. Then write down the few verses or even just a phrase that is making an impact. You may also want to record how it applies to what you're going through and note the encouragement that the Holy Spirit is whispering. You can also journal a prayer at the end—a personal response to what the Lord has said. He has spoken, so believe that you've heard His voice and act in faith by writing down what you've received. Writing gives us time to listen. It helps us get out of our own thinking and more clearly hear from God. It helps affirm what we're hearing and enables us to be deeply nourished by our daily bread. Rather than taking a word from the Lord lightly, journaling will help us appreciate and remember what God has spoken. Let's not take for granted the gift of our Father powerfully interacting with us in our daily lives!

When we conclude our time of meeting with the Lord in His Word, we can close our Bibles in peace, knowing that our mind and spirit has encountered the Person of truth (see John 16:13). Whether we "feel" different in the moment or not, we've been obedient, so we can trust that we're being transformed and equipped little by little, day by day, truth by truth.

This act of seeking the Lord in His Word with an expectant heart and responding in obedience makes an eternal impact on our mind, heart, and spirit. It's one of the most personal ways the Lord communicates with us. The more time we spend with Him in His Word, the more we know Him, recognize His voice, and learn His ways. Psalm 119 tells of the many benefits of learning the ways of God. Verses one through three are especially promising, "Joyful are people of integrity, who follow the instructions of the Lord. Joyful are those who obey his laws and search for him with all their hearts. They do not compromise with evil, and they walk only in his paths."

As we spend time with the Lord through reading His written Word, listening for the voice of His Holy Spirit, and writing what He says, we are changed. We receive what we need and are prepared for the challenges and decisions we'll face. And there's no need to worry, because the Holy Spirit will remind us of the things we've read and received (see John 14:26). Believing and keeping these things close, we gain strength and endurance for life. Faithful to feed on the Word of the Lord and spend this set-apart time with Him, He meets us right where we are. Through Scripture and the Holy Spirit, our Father imparts unconditional love, hope, correction, joy, and all the wisdom we could ever need. He will nourish, prepare, equip, and fill us each and every time.

Meditate

Is there anything holding you back from spending time with the Lord in His Word? Ask Him to help reveal what's blocking the way.

Will you commit to faithfully meeting with the Lord in His Word each day, with an open heart and mind?

Look for a Bible reading plan or checklist. "Read Scripture" is a great interactive app with a Bible reading plan and videos for each book of the Bible. Begin to read and journal about your time with the Lord in His Word.

Prayer

Father,

Thank You for Your written Word and the opportunity to really know You. I need Your wisdom and insight. I want to connect with Your heart. Give me a hunger for Your Word as I choose to make reading Scripture and hearing Your voice a priority.

"Open my eyes to see the wonderful truths in your instructions" (Psa. 119:18). Show me the places that are lacking Your love.

Holy Spirit, lead me and reveal the Father and the Son, through the written Word. Give me revelation that awakens my life to You! Help me to seek and find You, my Savior and closest friend.

Thank You, Lord, for faithfully revealing Yourself and Your truth within Your Word.

In Jesus' name, amen.

Chapter Nine

Time in Prayer

My heart has heard you say, "Come and talk with me."
And my heart responds, "Lord, I am coming."

—PSALM 27:8

T HE LORD IS CALLING us to a holy place where we abide with Him in prayer. We can participate in a large gathering or in a small group, but here, we'll focus on the prayer that comes from the lips of the individual, whispered while walking in the woods, sitting on a front porch, or communing from any solitary place. Our primary purpose in prayer is to share intimacy with our Creator—to know Him and be known by Him. It's to share our lives with Him, to give and to receive.

Prayer is a wonderful way to get to know the God who made us. It's where we express the devotion and appreciation we feel for our Creator. A place to be honest about our needs, prayer is where we lay down our burdens and pick up faith and hope. It's the way the Father works things out in us and brings about His plans. Prayer is where we receive the love of the Lord and experience His near presence. No matter what the enemy tries to tell us, there is great purpose in prayer. Let's receive a fresh appreciation for this meeting place and consider the many benefits that come from spending time with God in prayer.

We can learn a lot about prayer by looking at the way Jesus lived in the Gospels. He often went away to pray to His Father in a solitary place, many times on a mountainside. Our renewed vision for prayer is going to come from Matthew 6, where Jesus' friends asked Him to teach them about prayer. Let's listen to what He said and follow the model that He gave.

Jesus began by explaining that the meaning of prayer isn't about saying the right words or impressing God or others. In fact, it's just the opposite. He said, "When you pray, don't babble on and on as the Gentiles do. They think their prayers are answered merely by repeating their words again and again. Don't be like them, for your Father knows exactly what you need even before you ask him!" (Matt. 6:7–8). The Father knows us. He knows what we need, so it's okay if our words aren't just right. He wants us to come to Him, asking and trusting Him for our every need. In Luke 11:9–10, Jesus said, "And so I tell you, keep on asking, and you will receive what you ask for. Keep on seeking, and you will find. Keep on knocking, and the door will be opened to you. For everyone who asks, receives. Everyone who seeks, finds. And to everyone who knocks, the door will be opened." We seek and ask because that's what Jesus said to do. It's what He did when He walked the mountainside.

Like Jesus, we want to seek the Father alone, in a solitary place. Jesus taught, "But when you pray, go away by yourself, shut the door behind you, and pray to your Father in private. Then your Father, who sees everything, will reward you" (Matt. 6:6). This is the prayer Jesus modeled for us:

> "Our Father who is in heaven, hallowed be Your
> name. Your kingdom come; Your will be done on
> earth, as it is in heaven. Give us this day our daily
> bread. And forgive us our debts, as we forgive our
> debtors. And lead us not into temptation, but deliver
> us from evil. For Yours is the kingdom and the power
> and the glory forever. Amen."
>
> —MATTHEW 6:9-13 MEV

To pray like Jesus did, we separate from distractions and pause the things of life that press and pull. Like stealing away to a secret garden, we find a quiet place where we can let down our guard and freely interact with the Lord. Perhaps it's on a hillside, a sandy beach, or in a quiet corner of the house. In any such place, we go looking for the Father as a beloved child who cries out, "Our Father who is in heaven!" (Matt. 6:9). Papa God is close and ready to meet us, just as we are. We've come in need, immature in ways and a bit dirty from the earth where we live, yet His arms are outstretched, ready to greet His favored daughter, His favored son, with warm embrace.

Andrew Murray said, "Live as a child of God and you will be able to pray and most assuredly be heard as a child" (46). Free and trusting, we sing, speak, listen, cry, and laugh. Here with the Lord, we're free to express our devotion and love for Him. We're free to receive from our Father.

Remembering to magnify *His* name, *His* ability, we give God glory as we continue to pray, "Hallowed be Your name." The Passion Translation says, "may the glory of your name be the center on which our lives turn" (Matt. 6:9 TPT). Our Creator and Father is the One and only God. He sits on the throne above all, for all time, and we magnify who *He* is.

Hungry for so much more than this world can give, we cry, "Your kingdom come." We long for the King who reigns in heaven to rule in our hearts and lives and those around us, here and now. It's through you and me, His children, that the kingdom of heaven comes to the earth.

> *It's through you and me, His children, that the kingdom of heaven comes to the earth.*

Our asking ignites a desire for the supernatural things of heaven's realm that are unseen. God's kingdom is about righteousness, peace, and joy in the Holy Spirit (Rom. 14:17). The Voice translation says, "When God reigns, the order of the day is redeeming justice, true peace, and joy made possible by the Holy Spirit." This is what we want. This is the kingdom that we need on the earth! God, we welcome *You* to reign!

In a posture of surrender, we submit, "Your will be done on earth, as it is in heaven." We lay down our will and what we want, and we ask for God's will to be done. His ways are different than ours. We don't automatically think like Him or know what He knows. His perspective is so much greater than ours. He said, "'My thoughts are nothing like your thoughts,' says the Lord. 'And my ways are far beyond anything you could imagine. For just as the heavens are higher than the earth, so my ways are higher than your ways and my thoughts higher than your thoughts'" (Jer. 55:8–9). Needing His insight, we yield to trusting *His ways*. We ask for His will to be done, and then we allow Him to lead. Even when things don't make sense and it's hard to see how His plans can possibly be carried out, we keep praying according to His heart and ask for His plans in heaven to be done here on the earth. Then we trust Him to bring it about.

Our prayer of surrender aligns our priorities with His. The more we read His Word, the more we know His heart and understand His ways, so praying according to Scripture is another way to ask for God's will to be done. Jesus taught, "But if you remain in me and my words remain in you, you may ask for anything you want, and it will be granted!" (John 15:7).

Mindful that every good thing comes from our Father's hand we continue in prayer, "Give us this day our daily bread." Recalling His faithfulness in the past, with thanks we ask and trust that our Father will continue to provide. Our provider and source of life, the Lord wants us to talk to Him about all we need. Because of His omniscient vantage point, sometimes He does things differently than we think He should. It may be that He chooses to give us only enough for the day, like He did with His children in the desert when He provided manna one day at a time. Perhaps He wants us to lean closely, to know His heart more and to better trust His character. Whatever His plan and purpose, He will always provide and do it in a way that's best. Whatever provision we ask for, we can trust that He's a good Father who loves to give good gifts to His beloved children.

He knows what we require and reminds us in Matthew 6 not to worry, because He values each one of us. Let's really believe that this is true. He cares about even the smallest details and desires of our lives and loves for us to talk them over with Him.

Our Father has access to all we'll ever need and He waits for us to come to Him, trusting that He's ready and willing to give.

In our Father's generous presence, we find what we need, and we relish His acceptance. Because of His generosity we continue our prayer and confess, "And forgive us our debts, as we forgive our debtors." We have been fully forgiven! Let's celebrate this miraculous gift and give God thanks.

Jesus taught us to also forgive others. He said, "But when you are praying, first forgive anyone you are holding a grudge against, so that your Father in heaven will forgive your sins, too" (Mark 11:25). We have been forgiven of much, so we can extend the same gift of mercy that we've been given. Remembering the great mercy the Lord has shown, we release the accounts to set ourselves and others free.

Because Jesus chose to forgive, even in the most awful and unfair circumstances, we too can extend forgiveness, even when the cost is high. When we ask Him for help, *He will enable us* to release those who have caused us harm. Then He gives us a most beautiful gift—release from the bondage that unforgiveness brings. The Lord is truly free to do the miraculous among us when we agree to doing things His way.

Since we're not yet immune to temptation we pray, "And lead us not into temptation, but deliver us from evil." We're asking the Lord to help us recognize and resist the temptation the enemy offers. Our adversary is real and actively fighting against us, but when we ask for help, God will always rescue and show us a way out (see 1 Corinthians 10:13). He will help us recognize the voice of the evil one, so we don't have to follow or succumb to sin. The Lord leads us to a higher way. By setting our eyes on Jesus and abiding in Him, we resist. He is the Light that leads us to a beautiful life, and so much better than anything the enemy could offer.

Closing our prayer we remind ourselves once again that the Lord reigns and has a Kingdom that is far greater than what we see in the natural. We conclude, "For Yours is the kingdom and the power and the glory forever. Amen." The power is the Lord's. Everything we need is supplied by Him, and remember, He knows what we need! All that needs to be done, *He* will do, as we yield to Him. (Read Ezekiel 36:22-36 for greater understanding.) We can meet with our Father in the special place of prayer at any time. One day we'll see Him face to face, but until then, we can experience His kingdom, His power, and His glory here on the earth. Let us magnify the Lord with our lives and live to give Him glory for all the great things He has done!

What a treasure we have in this prayer of Jesus and in the example He set of going away to spend time with His Father in prayer. Although we have the freedom to speak with the Lord in various ways, this foundational prayer holds key elements worth repeating often. The Lord's Prayer helps us put our minds and hearts into a position of yielding and trusting the Father. There is power in submitting to the Lord and praying for His way. He is listening and responding to the trusting and obedient prayers of our hearts. Let's enjoy the communion that comes in prayer and carry it with us wherever we go. We can get away anytime and find our Father, ready to welcome, listen, and respond.

Meditate

Ask the Holy Spirit to help you receive new revelation and insights about praying the Lord's Prayer.

Search out a secret place. As you meet the Lord there, focus on God the Father welcoming you with a great big smile and arms open wide. Pray and enjoy the special bond that the two of you share.

Prayer

Thank You, Jesus, for teaching me how to pray.
"Our Father, dwelling in the heavenly realms, may the glory of Your name be the center on which our lives turn. Manifest Your kingdom realm and cause Your every purpose to be fulfilled on earth, just as it is fulfilled in heaven. We acknowledge You as our provider of all we need each day. Forgive us the wrongs we have done as we ourselves release forgiveness to those who have wronged us. Rescue us every time we face tribulation and set us free from evil. For You are the King who rules with power and glory forever" (Matt. 6:9–13 TPT).
Amen!

Chapter Ten

Connected to the Body

Carry each other's burdens, and in this way you will fulfill the law of Christ.

—GALATIANS 6:2 NIV

T HE LAW PAUL WAS referring to in the Scripture above is found in John 15 where Jesus said, "My command is this: Love each other as I have loved you" (NIV). We were made to love and be loved in face-to-face connection and our Father has planned the imperfect yet precise people to be a part of our community. Do you believe that our need for one another is a part of God's grand design? We might've gotten by with the comfort of the familiar found in family or close friends up to now, but to become all that God is making us to be, we'll need to go outside our circles and find encouragement, strength, and love from others who have battled and won the fights we now face. We need to connect with the people who will help our purpose come to life. The Lord has already placed these people in our paths to walk alongside us. Somewhere within reach is someone waiting to share their story, equipped to help show the way through. What if our complete healing and restoration, even our fulfillment and peace, hinge upon being connected to the body of Christ?

Being connected—becoming open and vulnerable in real relationships with believers like this can be challenging, especially if we aren't used to it. But if we want to receive the help that God wants to give, and experience the strength and joy of spiritual family, we'll need to release the pride of self-reliance and humbly accept His compassion and wisdom shared through the lives of others. Cultivating these close relationships can't happen if we only get together on Sunday mornings between ten and twelve, slipping in and out of pews. Smiling and saying once again, "I'm fine. How are you?" is like putting on a mask and holding up a shield. It keeps others at arm's length and our challenges safely tucked away. It seems safe, but living like this limits our healing and growth. It limits the peace and joy that comes through honest and connected living.

I was used to walking my path with a select few, none of which had been through the challenges I was facing at the time. Although I'd been advised to find a support group to deal with my fears and our family troubles, I struggled and resisted because I didn't want to admit that I needed help carrying my burden. But I desperately needed people to be real with, to lean on, and to learn from.

After trying different groups, we found help and hope in the emotional support program Celebrate Recovery. I mentioned in the first chapter what a place of safety this was for me, how people spoke openly about their struggles and didn't hide their fears or imperfections. There were no masks, no shields, just honest believers.

I was uneasy, at first, to be around people who were so free. They believed in God and set their hope on Him, while willingly wearing their humanity. They showed their frailty in spite of their fears. This wasn't always the experience I'd had with people at church. I'm not sure if it was from growing up in the South where we dress up and play good manners, or from not pursuing the people at church without putting up walls, or maybe I just wasn't ready. Whatever it was, pride was probably behind it. But when we put up walls we stay hidden and lonely.

The transparency at the support group allowed me, even required me, to drop the facade. Watching closely, they showed how to live sincerely and without shame, while believing and following Jesus.

Each week their openness was like an arrow directed at my heart compelling the question, *"What about you?"* Accustomed to keeping my fears and mistakes carefully hidden, I thought challenges and failures made me look like less of a Christian. I was afraid of exposure, shame, and rejection. But their example showed it was okay to be frail. They weren't scared away by my weaknesses and imperfections. They accepted me, even loved me, just as I was. Acceptance carried some of my load and helped my burden become lighter.

As I grew in courage and joined them in transparency, the fear that had a hold of me began to lose some of its grip. With time, our sacred Step-Study gatherings gave opportunity for the balm of forgiveness to reach the deeper hurts and replace them with love and truth. These people, the bravest of friends, the ones who were willing to humble themselves in honesty, made this exchange possible for me. It was beautiful and healing and so very freeing. I am forever grateful for their example of simply welcoming, listening, and loving, while freely sharing their own lives and shining the hope of truth.

In John 15:1–2 Jesus says, "I am the true grapevine, and my Father is the gardener. He cuts off every branch of mine that doesn't produce fruit, and he prunes the branches that do bear fruit so they will produce even more." Dead things hinder our growth and keep us from becoming, so the Lord must remove things like fear, jealousy, and shame, just to name a few. He wants to enable us to become what He first designed us to be. But we can't do it alone. We have to be in open, honest relationships for healing and growth to happen. We need to allow mature believers to speak to us honestly in love and we need to be willing to listen. It will likely be uncomfortable as we're learning to humble ourselves, open up, and rely on others. But with practice, we'll find this way of living to be freeing and true. We'll find that we also have much strength and encouragement to give.

Finding these friends made me hungry to live honestly and it taught me to look for others who were open too. In my looking, the Lord provided friends like family. They love Him and love me and help to show me the way. Willing to show their inadequacies, these brave women display God's redemption and speak of insight, correction, and encouragement. Through our honesty, we've built trust. That foundation holds us strong in challenging times. Ecclesiastes 4:9–10 says, "Two people are better off than one, for they can help each other succeed. If one person falls, the other can reach out and help. But someone who falls alone is in real trouble."

These are the friends I go to for understanding and counsel, to pray and help walk through forgiveness and healing, to help find God's truth. And when their burden is heavy, I help them walk through too.

In real relationships like this we don't expect perfection, but we do walk openly as we share the common goal of becoming like Christ. And we're committed to strengthening one another and lightening the load along the way. Sometimes I'm surprised by a weakness in a mentor, leader, or friend that I look up to. It's easy to build up a persona of perfection with such good friends. When we find that a friend

> *In real relationships we don't expect perfection, but we do walk openly as we share the common goal of becoming like Christ.*

or mentor isn't yet complete, it's just an opportunity to love without limits and readjust our expectations. If we're expecting perfection, then, at some point, we're going to be disappointed. Wouldn't it be better to see rightly instead, remembering that we're all in process of learning and becoming and are ever reliant on the Father? Then, we're free to extend the grace we've received, which covers all inadequacies. 1 Peter 4:8 tells us, "Most important of all, continue to show deep love for each other, for love covers a multitude of sins."

When weakness shows up, it's not up to us to tell others where they need to change. That's the work of the Holy Spirit.

Our role is to be connected through face-to-face relationships and be available for heart-honest dialogue, so we can function as the healthy body that God has designed us to be. This looks like getting together outside of Sundays and entering into one another's worlds. It's choosing humility and listening to the hard things without taking offense. It's thinking before speaking and saying what needs to be said. Speaking the truth at the right time and place, our motivation must always be love.

> *Real help and strength come through the body of Christ.*

Just as we have need for a safe haven in the family of God, there are sons and daughters, brothers and sisters, and mothers and fathers who want to be welcomed in too. They're waiting for someone to notice them, to see their value, and to give them room to be honest and valued. They may not even realize it yet, because it takes time to become aware of our need, but we all long for a place of acceptance, honesty, and contribution.

Each one of us needs to look for, find, and connect with the people God has placed in our path. Let's remember how suffocating it feels to wear a mask and be willing to go first in honesty. This is one way we put our love and faith into action, by building our relationships on truth and following Jesus together, just as Paul said: "Let the inner movement of your heart always be to love one another, and never play the role of an actor wearing a mask. Despise evil and embrace everything that is good and virtuous. Be devoted to tenderly loving your fellow believers as *members of one family.* Try to outdo yourselves in respect and honor of one another" (Rom. 12:9–10 TPT).

Real help and strength come through the body of Christ. Let's rely on the living church and take our place in the family.

Although we are incomplete and have much to learn, we are completely accepted and fully loved by our Father, just as we are. We have the freedom to be honest during the learning process and encourage others to do the same. While we walk with the Lord together, He's adding wisdom one layer at a time. And as these layers build, our maturity is being established. Together we're becoming strong.

Maintaining the health of our relationships within the body is a privilege and a responsibility. Participating in real friendships with other believers and stewarding those friendships well will result in a diverse, dynamic, and eye-catching community. Let's learn to lean on one another and realize the precious gift that the body of Christ truly is. As we help prepare one another for the return of our King, we will fully develop into the beautiful family the Father has designed us to be!

Meditation

Have you connected with people in the body of Christ that you can be vulnerable and open with? Are you willing to go outside of your circle of familiar family and friends to find the friends like family you are meant to walk with?

If you have these treasures in your life, thank God for them! And if not yet, then ask Him to show you who He's already placed in your path.

Prayer

Father,

Thank You for the people You've put in my life and for the way they love You and love me. I humble myself and receive the help that You've provided. Help me to take off the mask, to be open, so I can live whole and free.

I want to take my place in the body. Help me to function in a healthy way within the family and be a faithful friend. I express my love for You by loving others, so help me encourage and love the people in my community.

Holy Spirit, show me who to connect with! Help me to see others the way You do and be ever faithful to stewarding Your gift of community.

Thank You for loving me through Your family.

I love You too.

Amen.

Chapter Eleven

Remember the Cross through Communion

So Jesus said to them, "Truly, truly, I say to you, unless you eat the flesh of the Son of Man and drink his blood, you have no life in you. Whoever feeds on my flesh and drinks my blood has eternal life, and I will raise him up on the last day. For my flesh is true food, and my blood is true drink. Whoever feeds on my flesh and drinks my blood abides in me, and I in him."

—JOHN 6:53–56 ESV

APART FROM JESUS WE were needy wanderers without a home, separated from the Father and His provision. But we believe in the Cross and Jesus is our LORD, so we're joined to Him, covered by Him, and surrounded by God's acceptance and love. When the Father looks at us, He sees us through the glorious perfection of Jesus. He loves us with the love He has for His Son. So, He will never turn away from us, never shun or condemn us, because we're united with the Holy One. Our awareness of this unity is essential to walking in our new life, to becoming something vibrant! When Jesus spoke of our unity with Him in John 15, He explained that He is the vine and we are the branches—He is our source of life, so to live, thrive, and bless, we must stay connected to Him. Jesus urged, "Remain in me, and I will remain in you" (v. 4). So how do we remain in Jesus in an ever-present and on-going way? Like John says in the verse above, we can abide in Jesus by partaking of Him through remembering the Cross through communion.

According to the online Cambridge Dictionary, *communion* can mean, "a close relationship with someone in which feelings and thoughts are exchanged," as well as, "a Christian ceremony based on Jesus' last meal with his disciples" ("communion"). In previous chapters, the word *communion* has been in relation to the first definition, but for this chapter, we'll be referring to the last—to the cup and the bread that reminds us of Jesus.

The tradition of drinking the wine, or juice, and eating the bread, or cracker, usually takes place once a month within the walls of the church. One of the churches my family and I attended had a unique way of sharing communion. Once a month on a Sunday night, we'd gather together like a family and tables would be set up with baskets full of pita bread and large pitchers of grape juice. There was such a sense of freedom, and after we meditated on the meaning and prayed together, the pastor would encourage us to eat as much as we wanted!

Children especially enjoyed this tradition and would travel from table to table, cleaning up the leftovers. At the end of the night, we'd hold hands in a big circle and close by saying, "We love You, Jesus. We love You, Jesus. We love You, Jesus!" I think they were onto something pretty special!

Would you be open to receiving a fresh revelation of what communion means and consider bringing it into your daily life?

I want to challenge you to go beyond the ritual and formality, to find the freedom to bring the act of remembrance into your home, and to do so, often. It can be with family, or with friends when they're over for dinner, or on your own when it's just you and the Lord. Would you be open to receiving a fresh revelation of what communion means and consider bringing it into your daily life? Although there are other ways to stay connected with the Lord, I find that taking communion in my own home on a typical day helps me to remain in Him in a way like no other.

Let's picture the first communion when Jesus and His closest friends were sitting around a table, sharing a meal. We can find the story in Matthew 26; Mark 14; Luke 22; and John 13. Celebrating the feast of the Passover that day, they would have spoken about God's salvation in the past. They would've remembered God's protection and provision, given through the blood of a sacrificed lamb. And they would have celebrated how their ancestors found freedom from their bondage in Egypt. (We can read more about it in Exodus 11 and 12.)

Around that table and conversation, Jesus prepared to serve His friends a cup of wine and a loaf of bread. Picture Him looking into the face of each one as He broke the bread and said, "This is my body, which is given for you" (Luke 22:19). These men who trusted and followed Jesus, the ones whose feet He had just washed, were eager to partake in all that He had to give. They didn't fully understand the meaning, because they didn't yet know of the long night they were about to spend in the garden, a night of betrayals and beatings. They didn't yet know of their Lord's near suffering and death, or of the incredible victory and joy that would come three days later. And they were unaware of the trials and persecutions they would have to face, a price for following Him. They just knew Jesus and what He meant to them. And because they believed in Him (and He believed in them), they were willing to trust Him and receive in faith all He had to give. Picture them partaking of the bread that represented His body which would soon hang on a cross.

Imagine what these same men thought as the Lord then passed a cup of wine and explained that a *new salvation* was coming—that this wine represented a new covenant, or promise, that God was making with His people, right there, starting with them. Jesus lifted the cup and declared, "This cup is the new covenant between God and his people—an agreement confirmed with my blood, which is poured out as a sacrifice for you" (Luke 22:20). Matthew 26:28 adds, "It is poured out as a sacrifice to forgive the sins of many."

> *Like the lamb at Passover that was slain, Jesus was giving Himself as the perfect and final offering.*

Although the setting was informal, something remarkable and supernatural was taking place. The promise of a New Covenant between God and man, which had been foretold through the prophets Jeremiah and Ezekiel, was now being fulfilled by God! Like the lamb at Passover that was slain for the salvation of Israel and all the sacrifices God had required for the forgiveness of sins, Jesus was giving Himself as the perfect and final offering.

God explained the meaning of the blood to Moses, "for the life of the body is in its blood. I have given you the blood on the altar to purify you, making you right with the Lord. It is the blood, given in exchange for a life, that makes purification possible" (Lev. 17:11). For man to be made clean, for his sins to be forgiven, and for the miraculous New Covenant to be made, innocent blood had to be shed. God was about to supply the sacrifice that man could not give.

The Old Covenant had fulfilled what it was meant to do. Given from God through Moses to His people, it had shown the just requirements for sin; it told what was right and what was wrong, and ultimately, it made us all aware of our sinful nature and need for God. Because no son of Adam has ever been able to fully obey God's law.

In Galatians 3 Paul taught, "But those who depend on the law to make them right with God are under his curse, for the Scriptures say, 'Cursed is everyone who does not observe and obey all the commands that are written in God's Book of the Law.' So, it is clear that no one can be made right with God by trying to keep the law. For the Scriptures say, 'It is through faith that a righteous person has life.' This way of faith is very different from the way of law, which says, 'It is through obeying the law that a person has life'" (vv. 10–12).

Jesus was the only One able to obey God's laws, so He alone could offer a perfect sacrifice. Paul continues, "But Christ has rescued us from the curse pronounced by the law. When he was hung on the cross, he took upon himself the curse for our wrong-doing. For it is written in the Scriptures, 'Cursed is everyone who is hung on a tree.' Through Christ Jesus, God has blessed the Gentiles with the same blessing he promised to Abraham, so that we who are believers might receive the promised Holy Spirit through faith" (vv. 13–14). Jesus was bringing in a new and better way.

Through the life, death, and resurrection of Jesus, the New Covenant that had been prophesied was coming true. Through Jeremiah, God said, "But this shall be the covenant that I will make with the house of Israel after those days, says the Lord: I will put My law within them and write it in their hearts; and I will be their God, and they shall be My people" (Jer. 31:33 MEV). Instead of law etched on stone, God's finger would now write it on man's heart.

God has always wanted a people who would choose to love and obey Him. And what man has been unable to do since the very first in Eve and Adam, within the New Covenant, God promises to do. Our part is to abide and rely on Him. The author Andrew Murray concisely explains:

> In the first, man's desires and efforts would be fully awakened. He would be given time to prove what his human nature, aided by outward instruction, miracles, and grace, could accomplish. When his hopeless captivity under the power of sin had been discovered, the New Covenant came. In it God revealed how man's true liberty from sin and self, his true nobility and godliness, was to be found in absolute dependence on God. It was found in God's being and doing all within him. (19)

In the New Covenant promise, everything we need to draw near to God and be one who loves Him and lives an obedient life that honors and reflects Him, is supplied by God Himself. Absolutely everything that we require is found in God, and now, He is found within us who believe. Through Ezekiel, God explained how He would carry out this New Covenant:

> **Then I will sprinkle clean water upon you, and you shall be clean. From all your filthiness and from all your idols, I will cleanse you. Also, I will give you a new heart, and a new spirit I will put within you. And I will take away the stony heart out of your flesh, and I will give you a heart of flesh. I will put My Spirit within you and cause you to walk in My statutes, and you will keep My judgments and do them. You will dwell in the land that I gave to your fathers. And you will be My people, and I will be your God.**
>
> —EZEKIEL 36:25–28 MEV

This promise of our cleansing and receiving a new, tender heart, and having God's very Spirit living within is a promise and commitment from God—to us. *He will keep it.*

When we take communion we remember that we come to God empty-handed. We acknowledge our complete dependance on our King and remember His promise of provision. We remember the immaculate sacrifice of the blood and body of Jesus which speaks of empathy and holy kindness. His blood and body tell of forgiveness and the gift of new life. When we take communion, we're reminded that we have a heart that wants to obey God! And His Spirit lives within—always and forever. We are never left alone nor do we have to fend for ourselves.

Moment by moment, God is with us—guiding us, teaching us, and empowering us, supplying our every need.

Where we once had insecurity, He supplies boldness. Where there was unbelief, He gives faith. Instead of fear, He supplies trust. All of this and so much more comes within the Covenant that God has given in our new life. Whenever we take communion, we remember!

When you're ready, gather some plain crackers or bread, to represent the body of Jesus, and red grape juice or wine to represent His blood. This is how we will abide. Held within the bread is our remembrance of the Person of Jesus and how God became flesh for us—tangible, human, and vulnerable. Born as a baby like you and me, He lived a perfect life in an imperfect world. Although He was tested by trials and suffering, through His union with the Father He maintained a life without sin (see Isaiah 53 and Hebrews 4:15). He met the requirement of a spotless Lamb and was a sacrifice unto God on our behalf. It was His body that was beaten and bruised for us. It was His stripes that paid for our reconciliation and healing. Isaiah 53:5–6 communicates this truth to us: "But it was because of our rebellious deeds that he was pierced and because of our sins that he was crushed. He endured the punishment that made us completely whole, and in his wounding we found our healing. Like wayward sheep, we have all wandered astray. Each of us has turned from God's paths and chosen our own way; even so, Yahweh laid the guilt of our every sin upon him" (TPT). Now this perfect Lamb Jesus is raised to life and seated with the Father. Let's eat the bread and receive of all that God has given.

The wine is our remembrance of the sacrificial blood of Jesus and the power that it carries. It is the DNA of God and the only way to receive forgiveness for our sins. It is the only way to be welcomed into relationship with the Father—into God's family and into our new life. Perfect and holy blood was what our holy God required for our redemption and it is what has been given. The blood of Jesus covers the multitude of wrongs that we've committed, our actions as well as our thoughts, and it is enough to cover the sins of our past, present, and future.

In Hebrews 9:13–14 the writer explains, "Under the old system, the blood of goats and bulls and the ashes of a heifer could cleanse people's bodies from ceremonial impurity. Just think how much more the blood of Christ will purify our consciences from sinful deeds so that we can worship the living God. For by the power of the eternal Spirit, Christ offered himself to God as a perfect sacrifice for our sins." The blood of Jesus is more than enough to purchase our forgiveness, our salvation, and our reunion with God! His blood holds the promise of God's covenant. Let's drink of the cup and receive of all that God has given.

When we take the bread and drink the cup, we're reminded that His perfect life, death, and resurrection have paid the price for us to become new.

Everything that needed to be done for us to be made right with God has been done. Now when we take the bread and drink the cup, we're reminded that His perfect life, death, and resurrection have paid the price for us to become new. His death was counted as our death. His resurrection was ours. His ultimate victory is our victory. No matter what we face, Jesus' body and blood speaks triumphant.

Sin has been defeated and death has been conquered. Nothing can triumph the Cross. Because of Jesus, it is our final word. Through our remembrance, we meditate on the magnitude of what Jesus has done and we exalt Him. He is our LORD and standard against whatever comes against us.

When it's hard to believe that we're really washed clean, God helps us believe. Though the accuser whispers that our sin is too great, says we should keep it hidden, we must reject the idea and remember the price Jesus paid for our freedom. Through Isaiah God said, "'Come now, let's settle this,' says the Lord. 'Though your sins are like scarlet, I will make them as white as snow. Though they are red like crimson, I will make them as white as wool'" (Isa. 1:18). The blood of Jesus *is enough* to cover it all. Through the blood of Jesus, God washed us clean.

When it's hard to forgive, God enables us to forgive. The cup helps us remember that we've been forgiven and that the cost of our own salvation was unattainable. The highest price has been paid on our behalf. So, we lean on what we've received. We remember that justice belongs to the Lord and release hold of the accounts that tell of the wrongs done against us. We remember that while we were still sinners, Jesus died for us (Rom. 5:8). As we partake in communion, we receive the Lord's comfort and His love enables us to forgive.

Whatever we need for the challenges we face, Jesus has already provided for and made access to. Whether it's faith for restoration that seems impossible, trust instead of fear, forgiveness, healing, or any such miraculous thing, we can find it as we abide in the Lord. Let's join Paul in confidently declaring, "Yet even in the midst of all these things, we triumph over them all, for God has made us to be more than conquerors, and his demonstrated love is our glorious victory over everything!" (Rom. 8:37 TPT).

Jesus knew that we'd need help remembering, so He set a pattern for us. Just like He said to His disciples around the table, He's saying to us today—*Do this to remember me.* In order to remember, we have to abide, we have to lean on Him and remember that we are filled with Him. Like the friends who trusted and received from Jesus, we don't know what suffering or what joy is yet to come, but we do know our King. We know that Jesus has done what we could not, and we know how much God loves us. With our blessed perspective of looking back at the Cross, we know the deep meaning of the cup and the bread that represents the blood and body of Jesus in communion and we choose to remember and receive all that it holds.

Jesus set the first example of taking communion in a home. We can start the day with the cup and the bread on our own, or we can share it with friends and family around the evening table. What matters most is the attitude of our hearts and the desire to remain in Jesus—to stay connected to Him—and to keep the power of the Cross evident in our everyday life. Let's receive all the Lord has given and remember the Cross through communion.

Meditation

Gather plain crackers or bread, and red wine or grape juice, and prepare to remember the blood and body of Jesus, right in your home.

Prayer

Father,

Thank You for the gift of Jesus, the perfect Lamb who satisfied the punishment that I was due.

Jesus, You gave everything for me. You walked on the earth for me; Your body was tattered and bruised for me. You took on my humanity and sin so I could be forgiven and made right with the Father. You held nothing back.

I receive all that You are and all that You give. You are my daily bread, more than enough—all that I need. Jesus, You are life! Thank You. (Take the bread.)

Thank You for Your perfect blood that washes away the stain of my sin. Because of Your blood, I'm washed white, clean. I am in Your family! Your blood is my blood; Your body is my body. All that You are is available to me through the New Covenant, and I receive it now, in faith. Thank You. (Take the cup.)

I love You, Jesus. I love You, Jesus. I love You, Jesus!

Amen.

SECTION 3:
THE TOOLS
Filled & Empowered

**At last the wall was completed to half its height
around the entire city, for the people had worked with
enthusiasm.**

**But when Sanballat and Tobiah and the Arabs,
Ammonites, and Ashdodites heard that the work was
going ahead and that the gaps in the wall of Jerusalem
were being repaired, they were furious. They all made
plans to come and fight against Jerusalem and throw
us into confusion. But we prayed to our God and
guarded the city day and night to protect ourselves.**

**The laborers carried on their work with one hand
supporting their load and one hand holding a
weapon.**

—NEHEMIAH 4:6–9, 17

GREAT TRANSFORMATION IS TAKING place as we
abide in our champion King. His presence is permeating
through His Word and Holy Spirit, and we're ready to receive
and use all that He gives. We are ready not only to listen to God's

Word but also to do what it says (Jas. 1:22–25). Going on the offense, we are ready to protect and fight for our faith, our families, friends, and ourselves. We are ready to defend and take back stolen ground.

Although we don't always recognize it, the enemy is actively coming against us in the spiritual realm, and he doesn't give up easily. We're in a war with the unseen. Set your understanding to this truth: "For we are not fighting against flesh-and-blood enemies, but against evil rulers and authorities of the unseen world, against mighty powers in this dark world, and against evil spirits in the heavenly places" (Eph. 6:12).

In Genesis 4:7, the Lord God explained to Cain, "Sin, the predator is crouching in wait outside the door of your heart. It desires to have you, yet you must be its master" (TPT). The enemy is waiting just outside the door of our hearts too. He's offering temptations to believe his word instead of the Word of the Lord—to doubt, distrust, and disobey our God. Satan is trying to entwine us to him through our agreement with the fearful lies and temptations he offers. Like in the story of Nehemiah, let's continue to yield to our restoration and take part in the work, while staying alert and arming ourselves for spiritual battle.

There will be opposition. That voice might tell us to hold back, to play it safe, to protect ourselves. But we've come too far to listen to those lies. We've tasted perfect love and freedom and we know the truth: God is for us and He has gone ahead and prepared the way. The Lord has secured our victory no matter what the enemy says, and He is always near.

To stay faithful to the work of restoration at hand and be empowered to impact the world with light, we must utilize the tools the Lord has provided and take up the weapons He's given. We will not retreat and leave our work undone. Let's remain fully committed, while defending and laying claim to what is ours. Let's step into the next phase of our journey and take to heart the words of Nehemiah, "Don't be afraid of the enemy! Remember the Lord, who is great and glorious, and fight for your brothers, your sons, your daughters, your wives, and your homes!" (Neh. 4:14).

Chapter Twelve

Remember What the Lord Has Done

But watch out! Be careful never to forget what you yourself have seen. Do not let these memories escape from your mind as long as you live! And be sure to pass them on to your children and grandchildren.

—DEUTERONOMY 4:9

INSTEAD OF BEING SURPRISED when an attack occurs in the midst of our progress, let's stay mindful that the enemy doesn't stop fighting. We truly are in a war with things unseen. The adversary of our soul wants us to forget what the Lord has done in the past and focus on the current trouble. If we're forgetful, we can become easily overwhelmed by the latest harassment.

When disheartened and weary, we must strengthen ourselves by determining to look back at our Father's faithfulness. Remembering His hand of protection and the ways He's provided thus far sets our focus on Him and His ability. Rather than desperately hoping and relying on ourselves or others to save the situation, we fix our eyes on the only One who can. When setbacks come, to continue moving forward and higher, we must recall what the Lord has done.

Let me share from experience. Since finding support in community, things were progressing well in our home. One of our children had returned to relationship with the family and much restoration had taken place. Yet, when I found that we were facing another major setback, all the good that we'd experienced left my mind. My thoughts were flooded with frightening future possibilities. Although I'd prayed, believed, and spoken the truth in love, things weren't playing out as I'd hoped. The present disappointment loomed and hopelessness seemed to settle into every space of the room.

Sitting on the bedroom floor, I felt like hope was lost. It seemed as though we were going in circles, traveling the same well-worn path that we'd walked together for years. I had grown tired and weary of going this way. The disappointment I felt many times before had once again returned. Feeling the frustration and pain, I allowed myself to grieve. Because the Lord understands, I believe that He wept with me too.

What I had expected and hoped for was not yet my reality. I had to carefully consider how I would respond to the current trouble. I understood my reaction would greatly impact my future. If I focused on fear I'd be allowing the situation to lead me into greater depths of despair. I had gone that route before, but this time I chose to remember the Father's faithfulness.

Instead of focusing on what very well could happen, I began to recall what the Lord had done. He had mercifully provided protection in dangerous situations. He had brought people into our lives to love and support us and to help us keep holding onto faith. He had restored relationship with our child. The Father had done many remarkable things.

As I recalled one gift after another, I naturally began to thank Him. I reminded myself and the Lord of His faithfulness, and I asked Him to do it again. So here I was, faced with another opportunity to rely on Christ, the only One who heals broken hearts and restores lives. My perspective affected my thoughts, and my thoughts affected my actions. I turned away from despair and moved toward hope. The Father met me there and assured me that both my child and I were still in His hands and He was not finished yet.

We cannot allow our circumstances to control our emotions or behavior. As a Four on the Enneagram who feels all the feelings, this is an ongoing challenge for me! But, when we ground ourselves in the Lord, we can rise up in faith. Specifically recalling what the Lord has done in the past brings to mind His faithfulness. Recollection reminds us to ask Him to do it again and believe that He will, perhaps in a new way! It gives us opportunity to return and give thanks (like the *one* healed leper who came back to Jesus in gratitude in Luke 17:11–19). When we recall what the Lord has done, it's like pulling ourselves up from the battlefield and finding a strength we didn't know we had. As we speak the truth aloud and give the Lord recognition and credit for being God, we reset our focus and place our hope on Him. Let's turn our attention to Him:

> **Your unfailing love, O Lord, is as vast as the heavens;**
> **your faithfulness reaches beyond the clouds. Your**
> **righteousness is like the mighty mountains, your**
> **justice like the ocean depths. You care for people and**

**animals alike, O Lord. How precious is your unfailing
love, O God! All humanity finds shelter in the shadow
of your wings.**

—PSALM 36:5–7

I don't know about you, but I feel safe when things are work-ing out the way I want, like when life is comfortable. But the Lord wants us to know safety, even when life is hard, even when we have to wait or accept something different from what we expected. The expectation of a comfortable life makes us think we'll be free from suffering, pain, and sorrow. We're comfort-able with the familiar, with what we understand, and we like the feeling of being "in control." But that thinking is faulty. We can't hold onto life like a little idol in our hands, pretending to play King. Because we aren't the King and life is so much wider and higher and more mysterious than anything we can hold. I used to think that if I was good enough, I'd be protected from hard things. But that was never promised. In fact Jesus said, "Here on earth you will have many trials and sorrows" (John 16:33). If we're holding untrue expectations, then we're not thinking on what is true. We're setting ourselves up for disappointment.

If we're to endure hardships, how do we trust the Lord and keep hoping for good, even when it hurts and when we don't understand? How do we trust in the times of waiting? How do we keep from being swallowed up when things get desperate? We go back to John 16:33 to the rest of the verse where Jesus concludes, "But take heart, because I have overcome the world."

To overcome thoughts of despair, we must remain connected to the Lord. In connection, we can hear Him, feel Him, trust

Him, even when we don't understand. Psalm 145:17–20 says, "The Lord is righteous in everything he does; he is filled with kindness. The Lord is close to all who call on him, yes, to all who call on him in truth. He grants the desires of those who fear him; he hears their cries for help and rescues them. The Lord protects all those who love him."

I grew up hearing, "Be careful what you pray for." The insinuation was that God was waiting for opportunity to cause hardships, like He enjoyed watching us struggle. This perspective made me distrust His heart. But it's a lie. God is not that way. We can fully trust that His heart is good and full of love for us. His rod, mentioned in Psalm 23, is not for tripping or beating us, it is for protecting. He will not cause hard things and enjoy watching us struggle through them. In our pressing, the false form that the world tried to make us into is chipped away. Uncovering what we're made of, our Maker shows that we can beautifully reflect His image.

Our God is not a mean Father who pushes His children down or puts their hand to the fire to be able to say, "I told you so." He is kind and benevolent. He sticks close to us and walks beside us, closer than a brother. When He allows hard things to come, He stays near, whispering Fatherly wisdom, saying, *"I believe in you. You can do this. I've been here and I know the way through. I am here, right beside you."* And of our suffering, Psalm 56:8 contends, "You keep track of all my sorrows. You have collected all my tears in your bottle. You have recorded each one in your book."

Within the suffering, we have to believe our Shepherd is present and attentive and look for the treasure waiting to be found. How is He revealing Himself anew? Where are we growing stronger? What beauty is forming within the ashes? If this will be our perspective, then even in the sorrow and in the trial, we will be comforted and expectant for good. This is the mindset that our Father wants us to hold.

> *Within the suffering, we have to believe our Shepherd is present and attentive and look for the treasure waiting to be found.*

Although our battles continue, and there are mistakes and learning opportunities along the way, the truth is still the truth. The gains we have made still hold. The revelation and change the Lord has brought about has made an impact. Another failure does not eliminate success. It simply allows opportunity to humble ourselves again and gain a greater understanding of how Christ's strength works in our weakness. Paul explained, "Three different times I begged the Lord to take it away. Each time he said, 'My grace is all you need. My power works best in weakness.' So now I am glad to boast about my weaknesses, so that the power of Christ can work through me" (2 Cor. 12:8-9).

Mishaps don't mean that God has forgotten us or changed His mind. Even during the mess ups, the Lord's hand continues to be upon us and those that we pray for and love. We can trust that just as He's done in the past, He will continue to provide for and protect us even now. He will continue to work all things out for our good because we love Him and He loves us.

Yes, we've circled back around to a familiar place, a place we thought we'd moved past. But with each remembrance of the Father's faithfulness and with each step and decision to continue to believe and obey God, we advance! We are making progress. It may not look the way we thought it would. In fact, it's likely to be completely different from what we'd imagined, but God continues to work within the battle. In fact, Francis Frangipane explains, "The Lord incorporates delays into His overall plan: *delays work perseverance in us*. So crucial is endurance to our character development that God is willing to delay even important answers to prayer to facilitate our transformation" (37). The Lord is working and He will not stop now because He is faithful to complete what He's begun (Phil. 1:6). We get to be a part of bringing His plans to pass in our own lives and in the lives of others by believing in Him and what He says in His Word.

> *With each remembrance of the Father's faithfulness and with each step and decision to continue to believe and obey God, we advance!*

Exercising our faith by recalling the Lord's faithfulness is essential to receiving the promises He has for us. Let's strengthen our resolve by remembering the past and believe the Lord will continue to work on our behalf in the present and in the future. Our hope is in God alone.

In closing this chapter, remember that sometimes we need to rest in peace, away from the battle. We're not denying or ignoring the storm, we're simply experiencing it from a place of security and promise. To help, I want you to picture yourself standing on a hillside near the ocean. You're just outside the door of your dwelling, a home built within the side of a mountain rock. The skies are ominous gray and the winds are blowing, pushing your hair about. The rain is starting to wet your skin and you feel the reality of the storm. Although the assault is present, remember, at any time, you can retreat inside your home within the rock, where you will be safe and out of reach.

Like this dwelling place, the Lord is your Rock. Rest in His presence and spend time with the safe One. Sheltered by Him, feel the warmth of His fire and receive the refreshing that He serves. Tell Him about the wind and hear His promise of protection. Strengthened, you'll follow His footsteps, and see He's already gone ahead and prepared the way.

> For here is what the Lord has spoken to me: "Because you loved me, delighted in me, and have been loyal to my name, I will greatly protect you. I will answer your cry for help every time you pray, and you will feel my presence in your time of trouble. I will deliver you and bring you honor. I will satisfy you with a full life and with all that I do for you. For you will enjoy the fullness of my salvation!"
>
> —PSALM 91:14–16 TPT

Our refuge, Jesus, is here, always present and available. To experience His presence as our peace, we abide in His shelter. We remember what He's done in the past and our gratitude brings refreshing. He gives us a map of hope for the future, a light for the way, and His voice whispering go left, or go right.

Proceeding from this place of safety, we know that our Shepherd King always has a plan. Remembering has a way of strengthening us, glorifying God, and fortifying us for the road ahead.

Meditation

Do you need to retreat into the Rock for refreshing?

Spend some time recalling how the Lord has been faithful. You may even want to write out some of the memories, bringing to mind His faithfulness and love. Let the remembrance settle the truth that *He will remain faithful.*

Prayer

Father,

You have been faithful in many, many ways. I remember how You've protected and provided for me and those I love. I am so thankful. Help me, in my weakness, to lean on Your strength and trust in Your timing and Your ways.

You are always with me. Thank you for weeping with me in the suffering and disappointment. Help faith to grow as I continue to hope, pray, and believe You are working. You are a good, strong, and capable Shepherd and Father. I put my trust in You.

Thank You for leading me.

I am following You, Lord.

Amen.

Chapter Thirteen

Changing Our Minds to Celebrate

Be cheerful with joyous celebration in every season
of life. Let joy overflow, for you are united with the
Anointed One.

—PHILIPPIANS 4:4-5 TPT

O UR SPIRIT HAS BEEN made new, but our mind needs
time, training, and a whole lot of changing to catch up!
Going our own way has worn familiar tracks in our minds. To
be fashioned into a house where the Lord lives will take new
thinking and new thinking requires creating new paths. Often,
we're so comfortable with our own way of thinking that we don't
think much about it. But our thoughts—both the damaging and
the beneficial—greatly affect our lives in one way or another.
When we give room to regret and condemnation, discontentment, doubt, or fear, then at the very least, the negative thinking
distracts us and gets us sidetracked. At the worst, it consumes
and cripples us.

So, let's ask, to what harmful habits of thought have we
opened the door and welcomed into the home of our mind? And
why have we given darkness such room? Rather than dwelling

on anxious thoughts, we want to choose to rest in the Lord and celebrate what is lovely, holy, and true. Philippians 4:4 reminds us there is joy to be found in every situation, if we will only look for it. We can change our minds by remaining in God's presence and taking all things to Him in prayer, and by turning away from harmful thoughts and choosing to *focus* on the truth. It's a big task, but when we give our yes, the Lord makes it possible! Our Father wants us to honor Him by delighting in our days, so let's cultivate a life of contentment—even celebration—through the changing of our minds.

At the start of each year I like to ask the Lord for a new truth to focus on, and then listen for what He has to say. Throughout the months following, He unfolds layers of meaning through His Word and Spirit and teaches me to apply what He's speaking. A couple years ago I went to our local state park and stayed in a cabin with the purpose to get away and spend time with the Lord. Surrounded by solitude and trees and the Lord's presence, He spoke the word *celebrate* over me, like an exciting challenge and colorful opportunity to step into. He began to show me how often my mind settled onto things that caused me concern and how the time spent worrying made me miss the glorious gifts that were right in front of me. Like the people in our story of Nehemiah, our Father wanted so much more for me. He wanted me to enjoy the life He had given and to honor Him with my living. Learning to celebrate is an important part to becoming who God says we are.

It's a simple, but life-altering message that the Father wants to give you too, through the happy word *celebrate*! If you'll receive it, like I am, then you'll find that your mindset can be changed from worry to celebration. Philippians 4:4–8 (TPT) tells us how:

> **Don't be pulled in different directions or worried about a thing. Be saturated in prayer throughout each day, offering your faith-filled requests before God with overflowing gratitude. Tell him every detail of your life, then God's wonderful peace that transcends human understanding, will make the answers known to you through Jesus Christ. So, keep your thoughts continually fixed on all that is authentic and real, honorable and admirable, beautiful and respectful, pure and holy, merciful and kind. And fasten your thoughts on every glorious work of God, praising him always.**

Fear-provoking thoughts are not true, honorable, or lovely. I used to spend a lot of time worrying about the unpredictable and unknown things of the future. One day I was sweeping the floor when an idea of uncertainty snuck in and I started to play what our pastor calls the "what if" game. Playing this wager, the idea started to grow and gain momentum, even power, because I first gave it room in my mind. Before I knew it, I was consumed with anxiety and believed something awful was going to happen to my child—simply because I had dwelt on the negative *possibility*. My anxiousness convinced me that what I feared *could* happen, actually, probably would. Not only did I encourage myself to believe for the worst, but I even came to expect it. It engulfed my day, darkened my emotions, and stole my sleep.

Following fearful imaginations gives the enemy ground. It's drawing back and making room for darkness to dwell—to do what it wants. I wonder how much time and peace you and I have forfeited by worrying about things that have never come true, things the Father still holds in His hands.

Instead of following the trail of fear, we've got to stop giving the adversary access to impact our thinking. Let's remember the enemy loves to steal our peace and replace it with anxiety. We must reject his ideas to hold our ground and defend our peace. Just like changing a channel, we mentally move from fear to security by realizing that it's just a thought, just a suggestion sent to torment us from the evil one. The day that I was sweeping, when the Lord showed me my mind was dwelling on the negative, a lightbulb of understanding went on. I

> *Praying and proclaiming God's goodness (aloud) moves our mind to focus on Him.*

began to learn that we move from fear to faith by changing our thoughts. Instead of agreeing with worry and welcoming its effects, we pray to the Lord and declare peace, hope, and life. Praying and proclaiming God's goodness (aloud) moves our mind to focus on Him.

Jesus said, "I leave the gift of peace with you—my peace. Not the kind of fragile peace given by the world, but my perfect peace. Don't yield to fear or be troubled in your hearts—instead, be courageous!" (John 14:27 TPT).

Thoughts of regret don't honor God or the blood of His Son. Too often I've allowed memories of past failures to come haunting, carrying condemnation. When we allow them entry, we hold onto the heaviness of days gone by. Instead of carrying yesterday into today, we want to leave behind this habit of reminiscing on past regrets. We want to lay down our burdens of guilt and the former person we used to be. The enemy would love to keep us looking through the rubble and remain bound to our old man through regret, but the Father wants us to live like we're forgiven, fully free to enjoy today.

> *Once we've dealt with our past through repentance, it's time to stop digging through the debris.*

Once we've dealt with our past through repentance, it's time to stop digging through the debris. It's time to leave all the trash at the curb and let it go. When we repent and *receive* the Lord's forgiveness, then it's just as important to *believe* that we are forgiven. Changing our minds from shame to celebrating our new life in Jesus releases the hold of the past from affecting us anymore in the present.

The Father's shown us mercy for our sins and mistakes. We need to understand that in the past we were inattentive to the Lord and acting from our own faulty judgment and self-serving ways. It's not to justify our actions, but to allow ourselves to receive the mercy that we've been given. We weren't listening or following the voice of the Holy Spirit then, but we're listening now!

Let's silence the accuser with this word anytime he tries to speak anything different: *God, we thank You for Your kindness and mercy. I praise You for who You are and what You've done!* We celebrate the truth that our past regrets are no longer relevant!

Now, we're listening for what the Father has to say, and His Spirit helps us turn away from wrong. When we do make a poor choice, instead of allowing condemnation to sit in the mind, let's be quick to go to the Father. Remember, He doesn't think the way we do; He doesn't hold onto offense. He wants us to turn to Him like a trusting child and just be honest. We can tell Him we're sorry and know that He has already released it. We know He's released it because we have a faithful Father with open arms, and every mistake we've ever made or will make has already been covered by what Jesus accomplished on the Cross. Because of Jesus, nothing can separate us from the love of God. Let's celebrate this glorious truth by declaring with Paul:

> **And I am convinced that nothing can ever separate us from God's love. Neither death nor life, neither angels nor demons, neither our fears for today nor our worries about tomorrow—not even the powers of hell can separate us from God's love. No power in the sky above or in the earth below—indeed, nothing in all creation will ever be able to separate us from the love of God that is revealed in Christ Jesus our Lord.**
>
> —ROMANS 8:38–39

Let's honor the perfect sacrifice of Jesus and the loving heart of the Father by living free from the bondage of condemnation. Let's live in love, forgiven and accepted, freely enjoying our gift of new life.

While we're on the topic, have you ever gone to church and just as the worship begins, thoughts of condemnation rise up? They're so familiar I used to assume they were coming from the

Lord. I heard, "You're unclean. You can't go into God's presence, you have to get right first," as recent failures rushed to mind. These kinds of thoughts cause us to want to hide, to clean ourselves up and get right before being with the Lord. Before we know it, much of worship has been spent "getting right" with God rather than worshiping Him. What a clever tactic of the enemy. But we've been made new, so we *are clean*! We cannot allow condemning thoughts to keep us from our Savior's presence and from giving Him praise.

With a heart of appreciation for Jesus, we can stand in God's presence with grateful confidence as we worship with a pure heart. It may be helpful to prepare for times of corporate worship by spending time with the Lord before we go. That way, our minds are focused, and the enemy has no ground for distraction. We can also trust that the Holy Spirit will speak specifics when there's something we need to make right. Fully trusting Him, we are able to worship the Lord.

Sometimes, when our spirit responds to the Lord in thanks or praise, our minds catch on and question, "What are you doing? Who are you talking to? Do you really believe?" According to Romans 8:7 we should expect this struggle. It says, "For the sinful nature is always hostile to God. It never did obey God's laws, and it never will." This questioning is a battle for control between the flesh and our new spirit—another offer of sin waiting just outside the door. Fighting this battle is a part of the process of transforming the way we think.

When questions of doubt come, we just face them head on. There are different ways to do this, but I like to use the familiar hymn to remind myself and declare, "*I have decided to follow Jesus.*" And when I consider the question of leaving Jesus, like Peter, I reply, "Lord, to whom would we go? You have the words that give eternal life" (John 6:68). Truly, there is no turning back.

When the Lord spoke to me about celebrating, He included the topic of judgment, because it was one of those well-worn tracks in my mind. Judgmental thinking is not beautiful or respectful, merciful or kind. Instead of dwelling on differences and focusing on behaviors that rubbed me the wrong way, He wanted to teach me how to appreciate and celebrate the uniqueness He's given to each one of us—His children.

One day during worship, I was distracted by critical thoughts toward someone on the stage. The Holy Spirit kindly convicted me and whispered to turn my eyes and my attention away from them to focus on the Lord. It was so simple, yet it worked!

I'd struggled with seeing the good in others for many of my years, probably because I had a hard time believing that I had value just as I was. But the Lord is helping me to accept and celebrate others, and He's helping me believe that I'm accepted too. Instead of seeing the things that separate and make us different, I'm looking for the gold and finding that it's always there.

Recognizing and rejecting harmful thinking, whatever it is, and turning our thoughts and attention to the Lord helps us realize what an incredible God we have! There is ample opportunity to celebrate God's goodness. Instead of fear and worry, He gives trust and peace. Instead of regret and condemnation, God forgives and restores. Instead of fear and doubt, He helps us know peace and truly believe. Instead of criticism, He shows us beautiful things. These are changes worth choosing!

Changing our minds to appreciate the Lord and His goodness has a remarkable effect on us. Rather than living from a mindset of fear, worry, or lack, we live in a place of security and abundance. Not only do we have much to celebrate, we also have much to give. Through a life of celebration, we're free to focus on, appreciate, and love the people around us. And we get to extend an atmosphere of rest, acceptance, hope, and joy.

Let's live to honor the Lord by enjoying every good and perfect gift that comes from His hand and overflow

Through a life of celebration, we're free to focus on, appreciate, and love the people around us.

with thanks in every circumstance, through a life of celebration. James 1:17 reminds us, "Every good gift and every perfect gift is from above and comes down from the Father of lights, with whom is no change or shadow of turning" (MEV). The more we notice God's goodness, the better we enjoy the here and now. Good gifts—like a God who is for us, time on this earth with loved ones, the beauty of the world around us, stillness, a meal shared, and so many other simplicities are too easily taken for granted. As we slow down and value these treasures from the Lord, we can't help but receive more from Him, and in turn, we have more to give away. Somehow, the more we appreciate and share His gifts, the more we receive, and God's goodness never seems to run out.

Let's celebrate this life that the Lord has given by growing more mindful of our thoughts and changing our mind whenever harmful thinking comes. Paul instructed us in Philippians 4:4-8 to talk to the Lord about our troubles and to set our mind on what is true, honorable, lovely, holy, and kind. He said to fix our thoughts on God and to overflow with gratitude. That is what *celebrating* is all about!

Meditation

Are there any anxious thoughts on which you need to close the door? Any familiar tracks you need to replace?

What is something in your life right now that you can thank the Father for? You may even like to make a list. Think on these things!

Prayer

Father,

I've dwelt on negative thoughts far too often. They've caused me to be anxious and kept me from Your presence and peace. Thank You for revealing this to me. Holy Spirit, help me recognize harmful thinking as it comes. Empower me to close the door of my mind to darkness.

Thoughts of fear and insecurity have to go. Shame and regret from the past, you have no place here; you must leave.

I am clean, and I am new!

Father forgive me for being critical of others. Help me to see the beauty that You've placed within.

You have given so many wonderful gifts. Thank You! I'm grateful for Your salvation and presence, and for my gift of new life. Through celebration, You're making me more beautiful. You are a great Father and worthy of my thanks and praise. I choose to live a life of celebration with You!

In Jesus' name, amen.

Chapter Fourteen

Watch Every Word

**So may the words of my mouth, my meditation-
thoughts, and every movement of my heart be always
pure and pleasing, acceptable before your eyes, my
only Redeemer, my Protector-God.**

—PSALM 19:14 TPT

SINCE WE ARE GOD'S dwelling place, let's consider
words—the ones that we receive and the ones we send out.
Words are like birds, carrying messages of despair and decay, or
hope and life, so we want to give them thought. Messages leaving
lips are what we listen to and receive and believe—or reject. And
they're what we offer to others. They originate in the heart and
come through our mouth impacting our thoughts and actions
and affecting the lives of those around us. In Matthew 15:18 Jesus said, "But what comes out of your mouth reveals the core of
your heart" (TPT). We've been given a new heart, so let's catch
each word and determine if it's what we want residing within.
Let's decide if it's what we want to send out.

Starting with the words we listen to, let's be mindful of what
we allow in. Let's discern the words that carry despair before
they gain entry. Because darkness and light are both speaking,

we want to be careful of who and what we choose to give our time and attention to. Let's choose to listen to the sounds that let the light in.

Like guarding something precious, we must stop thieving words from coming in and stealing our belief and our peace. Instead, we must choose to hear words of life. Music, media, people, and literature can either move us toward despair or settle us into peace.

> *We must stop thieving words from coming in and stealing our belief and our peace. Instead, we must choose to hear words of life.*

Considering close influences, sometimes well-meaning friends will offer a word of advice, but if it goes against our foundation of Scripture it's not for us to receive. We want to be careful who we take our troubles to, because not everyone has our very best interest at heart. Not everyone knows the Lord or lives by His Word. If their words don't lead us along the path of life, then we don't give them entry, and we don't follow. The Holy Spirit will give us discernment about who to listen to; we just need to pay attention. Proverbs 4:23 explains, "So above all, guard the affections of your heart, for they affect all that you are. Pay attention to the welfare of your innermost being, for from there flows the wellspring of life" (TPT).

So, who should we let in, and who can we trust? We can use these questions to help us determine the answer: Do they have a close relationship with the Lord? Do they value and read His Word? How do they treat others? Does the fruit of their life

demonstrate growth and maturity? Kind, trustworthy, and spiri-
tually mature people are usually the ones we can trust and allow
to speak into our lives. Remember your value and guard your
peace as the Holy Spirit helps you decide.

Also considering the words we speak, when teaching on the
tongue James said, "Sometimes it praises our Lord and Father,
and sometimes it curses those who have been made in the image
of God. And so blessing and cursing come pouring out of the
same mouth. Surely, my brothers and sisters, this is not right!"
(3:9–10). Think about that—we praise God, and with the same
given breath, we criticize the ones
that He's made. With appreciation for
the power that our mouth holds, let's
think about how we can resist cursing
and use our words to be a blessing.

> *We can choose
> to see and
> speak like God.*

When the enemy whispers fear, comparison, or judgment,
instead of speaking it to life, we can put the deceiver's voice to
death by coming out of agreement with his ideas. We can choose
to see and speak like God instead. The Lord has a lot to say
about how we act toward one another. He says we all have value
because He's fashioned us each one with His hand (see Psalm
139:13). He says in Jesus we are made completely new (see 2
Corinthians 5:17). He says to be kind and quick to forgive one
another (see Ephesians 4:32). And He wants us to give others
the patience, encouragement, and mercy that we would like to
receive (see Matthew 7:12).

My longest lifetime friend taught me something valuable
years ago, and I've tried to live by it ever since. She says that

when we think something nice about someone, even if we've just met, that we should say it, and we should give it! This spreading of joy is a fun way to bless!

To have a deep well of life-giving words to draw from we can fill ourselves with the insight, wisdom, and strength that's found in God's Word. God says, "Fill your thoughts with my words until they penetrate deep into your spirit. Then, as you unwrap my words, they will impart true life and radiant health into the very core of your being" (Prov. 4:21–22 TPT). Once we know the truth, then we can also give it away.

We can also speak Scripture aloud to fight our battles.

God's Word will always accomplish what He wants it to do. Through Isaiah, God said, "So also will be the word that I speak; it does not return to me unfulfilled. My word performs my purpose and fulfills the mission I sent it out to accomplish" (Isa. 55:11 TPT). Partnering with God in prayer and speaking His Word declares Him as Lord. It reminds us of the benevolent and mighty God we believe in. It's joining our breath, our voice, and our focus on what our God has said to be true. Giving Him our agreement and bringing His plans to life with our words is the way that God has chosen to move.

So we simply ask, and the Holy Spirit will lead us to specific promises in Scripture to pray for every situation. He'll highlight something to hold onto and hope for, and to declare until it comes to pass.

There are some Scriptures I've been holding onto and declaring for years. I've chosen to take God at His Word and I can see that He's working. Sometimes the Lord will also give us a picture to help us pray and believe. The Lord once showed me one of my children sitting cross-legged, covered in unlocked chains. It was a representation of what was happening in the spiritual realm that directed me to pray and declare freedom over their life. Agreeing with John 8:36, I declared that my child *has been* set free! I began to pray for them to rise up out of those chains and to walk in their freedom. It is happening!

Whatever form God's promise comes in—through Scripture or inspired imagination, we bring it to life by praying and speaking it aloud. Just like I declared freedom over my child, in prayer we declare God's truth aloud. Why out loud? Because thinking is not the same as speaking. Remember, God spoke, not thought, the light into being (Gen. 1:3). Jesus spoke the Word to the devil when He faced temptation in the wilderness (Matt. 4:1–11). In Ezekiel's vision of the valley of dry bones, the Lord told him, "Prophesy over these bones, and *say* to them, O dry bones, *hear* the word of the Lord" (Ezek. 37:4 ESV, emphasis added). Our revelation from the heart of the Father will be like a life-ring that secures and sustains us through the storm. Let's use it by declaring aloud God's promises until we see them come to pass.

The Lord, His angels, the demons, and the accuser are all listening. Our own ears are listening. Our minds are paying attention to the spoken word. The Lord told Ezekiel to *prophesy* according to what God said—to speak something that was not as though it was. This is what we're doing when we're faithful to speak the Word the Lord gives us. We're trusting in what *He sees.* We're exercising our faith by putting our heart, thoughts, and words into alignment with His. We are prophesying the promise that our Father is faithful to bring to pass.

In his small, but mighty book *God's Creative Power*, Charles Capps teaches, "Words are containers. They carry faith, or fear, and they produce after their kind" (5). Every message we utter is carrying the seed—the potential for death or life, fear or faith. It either carries darkness that drains hope, or light that awakens magnificent possibilities.

We'll conclude with the words of James that teach us how to watch every word, "But the wisdom from above is first of all pure. It is also peace loving, gentle at all times, and willing to yield to others. It is full of mercy and the fruit of good deeds. It shows no favoritism and is always sincere. And those who are peacemakers will plant seeds of peace and reap a harvest of righteousness" (Jas .3:17–18). God's wisdom is what we set our mind on, what we fill our heart with, and what we allow to leave our lips. It's what we meditate on and listen to. Following His way, we are promised a beautiful reward.

Let's let faith alight on the wings of our words. Watching each one, we honor the Lord, protect our peace, bring forth the light, and participate in bringing blessings to life.

Meditate

Are there any sources of words that are robbing your peace and belief? Are there any voices that you don't need to hear?

What revelation of God's wisdom is He leading you to align with and send forth in declaration?

Prayer

Father,

I confess that my words haven't carried light and truth as often as they should. I repent for speaking things that brought doubt and death instead of hope and life. Help me to weigh my words with Your wisdom. Help me, Holy Spirit, to honor and bless with my words today.

Holy Spirit, lead me to Scripture that applies to what I'm going through. I will hold onto the promise and declare it in faith, believing You will bring it to pass in Your perfect time.

I trust You. I honor You. I love You.

In Jesus' name, amen.

Chapter Fifteen

A Life of Worship and the Gift of Praise

From now on, worshiping the Father will not be
a matter of the right place but with a right heart.
For God is a Spirit, and he longs to have sincere
worshipers who adore him in the realm of the Spirit
and in truth.

—JOHN 4:23–24 TPT

I T'S HARD TO PUT an act of the heart into words, but we worship not only when we gather to honor God with a group but also on our own, in the quiet humbling of our hearts throughout each day. Worship is a continual heart-keeping, a progressive purifying, and a relentless responding in connection. It's cooperating with our mind being renewed, on an ongoing basis. A life of worship is appreciating and glorifying our King by enjoying and stewarding the breath, relationships, talents—natural and spiritual, and all we've been given. This connection of admiration allows us to be a container for the glory of the Lord.

As a creation made to worship, we can wonder—who has the Maker designed me to be? What potential has He envisioned?

Why has He placed what I have within my hands? To ask these questions, and to listen, receive, and respond is to make our lives fully available to worship, whatever we do. Let's consider what a life of worship looks like and enjoy responding with the gift of praise.

In her book about worship titled, *Glory*, Ruth Ward Heflin teaches, "God wants to awaken your heart to love. He wants to awaken your heart to adoration. He wants to awaken in you the ability to worship him" (128). We are being awakened! We are becoming a creation that worships in spirit and in truth.

> *We are being awakened! We are becoming a creation that worships in spirit and in truth.*

In *How to Worship a King*, Neese explains, "Worship is the opposite of religion. The heart of worship says, 'Jesus proved I am of value to God. I serve Him because He is also of value to me'" (4). He asks a question that we, too, want to ponder, "What would happen to your life if you began to focus every aspect and decision on ministering to God?" (16).

Loving God through a surrendered life is our main ministry. Living loved and sharing this love with others follows closely behind.

To me, this ministry of worship begins with appreciating the Lord. Stewarding our lives from a thankful place touches everything. When we wake up in the morning and set our mind on the connection that we share with the Trinity, we have an awareness that we've received the gift of another breath, a fresh start, and God's glorious near presence. A friend shared a happy way to start the day; she taught me to say, *"Good Morning, Father! Good Morning, Jesus! Good Morning, Holy Spirit!"* Many mornings I enjoy setting my mind on God this way, including Him from the very beginning.

A grateful life of worship teaches us to see things differently. It helps us notice the people God has placed in our lives and appreciate their value. Instead of comparison or judgment, we look for their worth and call it out when we see it. Instead of wishing for what we don't have, like a new car or bigger home, or different city to live in, we appreciate the safety, warmth, and comfort provided by what we do have. This is living with an attitude of abundance! Rather than pining for more, we can be content with who we are, where we are, and with what we have, and we can use it all to honor the Lord!

Wherever God has placed us and whatever He has given, we can worship by appreciating and stewarding our lives well. Going about the day—folding laundry, patiently loving and training our children, or giving our best at work are a few of the simple ways we steward our lives with worship. We worship while we're working with excellence and treating others with respect. We worship when we pay our bills on time. We worship by doing it all unto the Lord. Let's live by this truth, "Put your heart and soul into every activity you do, as though you are doing it for the Lord himself and not merely for others. For we know that we will receive a reward, an inheritance from the Lord, as we serve the Lord Yahweh, the Anointed One!" (Col. 3:23–24 TPT).

We worship when we deny selfishness and choose submission. We worship by making the presence of Jesus our priority.

Honoring Him moment by moment is an ongoing sacrifice. The Apostle Peter taught, "So you must live as God's obedient children. Don't slip back into your old ways of living to satisfy your own desires. You didn't know any better then. But now you must be holy in everything you do, just as God who chose you is holy. For Scriptures say, 'You must be holy because I am holy'" (1 Pet. 1:14–16). Choosing holiness is a sacrifice, but since Jesus paid such a high price for us, isn't He worth our worship? Pursuing His presence and becoming like Him is our aim and desire. Becoming holy like He is, is a way to worship.

Wherever we go, God is with us. Who we are becoming, it is by His design. All we have, He has given. So, in everything, let's give glory to the King and be beacons of His light! We're made to be light, not to be hidden, but to shine! Jesus said, "You're here to be light, bringing out the God-colors in the world. God is not a secret to be kept. We're going public with this, as public as a city on a hill. If I make you light-bearers, you don't think I'm going to hide you under a bucket, do you? I'm putting you on a light stand. Now that I've put you there on a hilltop, on a light stand—shine!" (Matt. 5:14–16 THE MESSAGE). God has given us the go-ahead to shine brilliantly!

> *God has given us the go-ahead to shine brilliantly!*

Growing brighter and brighter, our light dispels darkness. It heals the brokenhearted and sets the captives free. Our light does marvelous things, and it first begins with an awareness of worshiping God in the small things and honoring Him in our everyday lives.

What about the times when a response of worship does not come easily? What about when we're hurt or offended, and worship is the last thing we want to do? If we'll choose to humble ourselves and take time with Him, the Lord will help us. When we choose surrender, our worship will be so much more than just a song in a pew. Because Jesus said, "So if you are presenting a sacrifice at the altar in the Temple and you suddenly remember that someone has something against you, leave your sacrifice there at the altar. Go and be reconciled to that person. Then come and offer your sacrifice to God" (Matt. 5:23–24). God wants us to not only bring a sacrifice of worship at church on Sundays, but to also faithfully live according to His heart, every single day. We worship when we turn away from anger, bitterness, and offense. And we worship when we forgive and show love out of the abundance of goodness that Jesus has shown. When everything is done unto the Lord, the way we live is our worship, and it's an on-going offering to our beloved King.

First John 3:11 says, "We should walk in self-sacrificing love toward one another" (TPT). This humble way of walking looks like resisting offense, seeking to understand, and extending mercy, even when it's underserved. It might look like staying quiet, instead of presenting a defense (this one is especially hard for me), or denying our flesh by saying, "I'm sorry," when we don't yet want to. It's forgiving and letting things go—again and again. It's turning to the face beside us and giving the very mercy that we've been given.

So much more than ritual, God wants our hearts to be right before Him by living out His ways in our day-to-day lives. I'm so thankful that the Lord allows room for our struggling and mistakes. What He cares about most is the attitude of our heart. Let's respond as God desires—let's live out the law of love. In appreciation, all that we do, although imperfectly, can be a gift for our King. For this is a lifestyle of *true worship.*

Living a life of worship makes us more aware of the Lord; we realize how involved He is, how incredible, how perfect and kind. Naturally, we must respond with praise, or we'll burst! We have to let God know how we feel about Him! We were created to respond, and our praise is a gift that you and I can uniquely give to our King. It is another act of worship, a physical response to glorify our beautiful and mighty King—demonstrated well by King David, the man after God's own heart.

Perhaps we'll respond like David in song, "I will be filled with joy because of you. I will sing praises to your name, O Most High" (Psa. 9:2). Maybe we'll dance like David, "And David danced before the Lord with all his might" (2 Sam. 6:14). Or lift our hands, "Lift your hands toward the sanctuary, and praise the Lord" (Psa. 134:2). We may kneel in honor, "Come, let us worship and bow down. Let us kneel before the Lord our maker, for he is our God" (Psa. 95:6–7). Or clap and shout, "Come, everyone! Clap your hands! Shout to God with joyful praise! For the Lord Most High is awesome. He is the great King of all the earth" (Psa. 47:1–2).

The Lord is truly worthy of any one of these expressions of praise and adoration. He is worthy of our personal response. Why would we withhold anything from Him? God has been faithful to pour out His love throughout our lives, like falling waters, always refreshing and running down. We've drunk deeply of His love. Now let us return it in our praise!

God is worthy of our adoration, no matter what we're experiencing. There's always reason to give God praise. Even in sadness—when we're disappointed, hurt, and tired of waiting, and while the tears are still on our cheeks, we can still praise, because the truth hasn't changed. God is still for us and with us. He is still a good and faithful God. We can be honest with Him, feel what we're feeling, and yet, give Him praise.

I believe this is an exceptional and sacred sacrifice, one that creates a pleasing offering to the Lord. Like incense going up, our praise mixed with tears reaches the heart of our King and connects us closely with Him. Our tender and loving Father is moved when through the pain, we still honor Him as LORD.

Our praise sets the atmosphere. It attracts the Lord's presence and His weighty glory. When we need our emotions to move from despair and worry to

> *Our praise attracts the Lord's presence and His weighty glory.*

hope and trust, we can praise. We begin by humbling ourselves and lifting up the name of the Lord. We set our mind on Him and honor Him above the circumstance. Defeat cannot stand in the presence of our praise because God is there. His perfect love sends fear and worry running. It brings hope and confidence to our souls, reminding us that God holds us secure. So, when we don't feel like it, that's when we need to do like David did and *tell our souls* to *bless the Lord!* Sometimes our actions need to lead and then our emotions will follow.

The psalmist David, a child of God who was not ashamed nor afraid to express his love for the Lord, admonishes you and me:

> **Lift up a great shout of joy to the Lord! Go ahead and do it—everyone, everywhere! Worship As you serve him, be glad and worship him. Sing your way into his presence with joy!**
>
> **And realize what this really means—we have the privilege of worshiping the Lord our God. For he is our Creator and we belong to him. We are the people of his pleasure.**
>
> **You can pass through his open gates with the password of praise. Come right into his presence with thanksgiving. Come bring your thank offering to him and affectionately bless his beautiful name! For the Lord is always good and ready to receive you. He's so loving that it will amaze you—so kind that it will astound you! And he is famous for his faithfulness toward all. Everyone knows our God can be trusted, for he keeps his promises to every generation!**
>
> —PSALM 100:1–5 TPT

A few years ago, I visited Dallas to take part in a conference where worshiping the Lord was a priority. Singing with the many voices in the auditorium one afternoon, I knew things were happening in the spirit realm, things that were not seen.

While worshiping with thousands of others, our surroundings became charged with the Lord's powerful presence. I felt prompted to ask the Lord what He wanted to give to me. In my spirit, I saw a golden sword coming down from heaven. He was teaching me that praise is also used for battle. Our praise was piercing the darkness and welcoming in the light.

As we moved into prayer against fear, a woman praying for me acted out removing arrows from my back. What she didn't know before the Holy Spirit led her to pray this way was that I'd been so fearful of frightening possibilities that it seemed my life was littered with such shots. Our praise and prayer facilitated the removal of the enemy's debilitating darts. It made room for the light, which always expels darkness.

There's a story in 2 Chronicles 20 that shows the power of the weapon of praise. King Jehoshaphat was leading the people of Judah at that time, when he heard a huge army was heading their way. He sought the Lord and told the people to fast and pray. Jehoshaphat prayed, "Whenever we are faced with any calamity such as war, plague, or famine, we can come to stand in your presence before this Temple where your name is honored. We can cry out to you to save us, and you will hear and rescue us" (20:9). He continued, "We do not know what to do, but we are looking to you for help" (v. 12).

The Lord heard their prayers and sent the message, "Do not be afraid! Don't be discouraged by this mighty army, for the battle is not yours, but God's" (v. 15).

The people responded in praise and worship, believing their God and trusting in Him. They felt led to have singers lead the way in battle, praising God "for his holy splendor." Going first, they sang, "Give thanks to the Lord: his faithful love endures forever!" (v. 21).

The moment the singers began to praise, the opposing armies started fighting one another. The Holy Spirit does this kind of work. By the time King Jehoshaphat's army got to the battlefield, their enemy was already dead. God had been true to His Word.

In our praise, our Father fights for us.

When trouble looms large—consuming, and the enemy challenges us to the very core, it can seem impossible to lift an offering of praise. But in spite of uncertainty and anguish, we must press into praise, declaring the goodness and faithfulness of our God. It's not denying our feelings or the facts but trusting our Father to fight for us and rescue us once again. Praise reminds us of the truth; it realigns our thinking and enables us to remember how mighty and full of light God is. Our praise calls forth the light and prepares the way for the battle to be won.

Praise moves our eyes from what we see in the natural into the realm of the impossible!

Praising before we see the breakthrough is like going ahead and marking out the territory. It's claiming our victory that is yet to come. The Lord has given us praise to use for battle, and He's gone before us and already won. He's put a sword in our hands, and it is the gift of praise. Our enemy hates it. The Lord God Himself inhabits it.

Every time we enter the King's presence with our praise, setting our thoughts on Him, we glorify Him, praising Him for His faithfulness and love. In these moments, His joy really does become our strength. Praise moves our eyes from what we see in the natural into the realm of the impossible! Praise pushes us past our present and declares something better for the future. And it glorifies God, giving Him the honor that only He deserves.

We cannot leave our song unsung. Heflin inspires us by saying, "your worship is distinctive. It is uniquely 'you.' It touches the heart of God" (118). Let's touch God's heart—through a life of worship and the gift of praise!

Meditation

How is the Lord encouraging you to make worship and praise a lifestyle?

Read Psalm 34 aloud. Add your own words of praise and send them into the atmosphere. Give God glory as you declare victory and call forth change!

Prayer

Father,

Thank You for my life; I want it to be an ongoing song of worship. Help me appreciate and steward well Your many gifts. Help me honor You moment by moment, day to day, with a life of worship.

I was made to give You praise! It's a joy to sing of Your goodness and faithfulness and to give You glory.

Engaging this gift reminds me that You are fighting for me. My eyes and my hope are on You as I anticipate our victory!

What a beautiful gift praise is. It takes me into Your presence, the place that I love. My heart can't help but respond—Praise the Lord!

In Jesus' name, amen.

Chapter Sixteen

Led by the Spirit

For the Lord is the Spirit, and wherever the Spirit of
the Lord is, there is freedom. So all of us who have
had that veil removed can see and reflect the glory of
the Lord. And the Lord—who is the Spirit—makes us
more and more like him as we are changed into his
glorious image.

—2 Corinthians 3:17–18

IT IS BY THE Spirit of God that we're transformed into a
life made beautiful, made into a new creation and built up,
strong and complete. Paul explained, "The mature children of
God are those who are moved by the impulses of the Holy Spirit"
(Rom. 8:14 TPT). When we're moved by the Holy Spirit and welcome Him to lead, we can yield to the Father's hand, become
His design, and live out His purposes for us. The apostle Paul
explains how this works, "Who can see into a man's heart and
know his thoughts? Only the spirit that dwells within the man.
In the same way, the thoughts of God are known only by His
Spirit" (1 Cor. 2:11 THE VOICE). The Father shares His thoughts
with us through His Spirit. We must be open to this mystery because without the Spirit of the Lord we cannot rightly perceive
the heart and mind of God. Paul continued, "But a person who

denies spiritual realities will not accept the things that come through the Spirit of God; they all sound like foolishness to him. He is incapable of grasping them because they are disseminated, discerned, and valued by the Spirit" (v. 14). It is *by His Spirit* that we know God and experience the delight of all He has for us.

To be led by the Spirit means to honor and trust God's ways more than our own. It is to welcome the Lord in every area of our lives and listen to His voice. The Spirit leads us to choose the narrow path, the way not widely traveled, because we've been set apart and made holy. This path holds peace and joy, as well as some suffering. The Holy Spirit leads us this way according to the Father's will, so even though there's challenge, we must follow, we must go, knowing He is with us, and in the end, His way leads to eternal life.

> *The Holy Spirit is the One who represents and reveals Jesus to us.*

To walk with us, the moment we believed in Jesus we were given the gift of the Holy Spirit. But as mentioned in chapter 7, we either welcome and include Him fully, or we ignore and reject Him, even as a Christian. As for me, I found that I needed the presence of God through His Holy Spirit, that I couldn't walk His way without Him. I needed His voice in my life, His constant comfort, wisdom, and leading. I needed Him to enable and empower me to live in a way that pleased the Lord and brought about peace. When I welcomed Him and asked Him to come, I realized God *was* close. He opened my eyes to see and my ears to hear and softened my heart to receive God's empowering presence.

Now I realize that it's the Holy Spirit who's been with me all along—since I believed as a child. He is the One who represents and reveals Jesus to us. It's His whisper that we hear in a supernatural thought or impression that speaks of love, wisdom, and direction. The Holy Spirit makes God's presence known; He is the One we feel.

He is the gift of the Father on the earth, fully available to all of God's children. Jesus said, "I will talk to the Father, and he'll provide you another Friend so that you will always have someone with you. This Friend is the Spirit of Truth. The godless world can't take him in because it doesn't have eyes to see him, doesn't know what to look for. But you know him already because he has been staying with you, and will even be in you!" (John 14:16–17 THE MESSAGE).

When we welcome the Holy Spirit and invite Him to lead, He will help us in every way. There is so much joy to be discovered by living a life led by and filled with the Spirit of God. Let's consider some of the greatest joys.

He helps us walk as a child of God. No longer led by the heaviness of the Law, now we are sons and daughters, free to live by the law of love—by the Holy Spirit. His way is light and gentle, like a dove. He woos us by showing us the goodness of God. And He helps us to believe and receive God's love, and to give it away.

The Holy Spirit enables us to know and follow the Lord by unlocking the mysteries of Scripture and enlightening us with revelation. He takes the beautiful truth of God and reveals how it applies directly to our lives. Jesus explained, "But when the Spirit of truth comes, He will guide you into all truth. For He will not speak on His own authority. But He will speak whatever He hears, and He will tell you things that are to come. He will glorify Me, for He will receive from Me and will declare it to you" (John 16:13–14 MEV). The Holy Spirit teaches us, and when we need to remember what we've learned, He reminds us of the truth. Jesus explained, "But when the Father sends the Advocate as my representative—that is, the Holy Spirit—he will teach you everything and will remind you of everything I have told you" (John 14:26).

> *The Holy Spirit enables us to know and follow the Lord by unlocking the mysteries of Scripture and enlightening us with revelation.*

The Holy Spirit enables us to become like Jesus. He shares His own traits, and as a good gardener, causes them to grow in us like fruit within, making us more like Him. The Lord is astonishing, and we want to be like Him! Imagine becoming who God says we are. Receive this truth within: "But the fruit produced by the Holy Spirit within you is divine love in all its varied expressions: joy that overflows, peace that subdues, patience that endures, kindness in action, a life full of virtue, faith that prevails, gentleness of heart, and strength of spirit. Never set the law above these qualities, for they are meant to be limitless" (Gal. 5:22–23 TPT). This picture of God reflecting in us isn't a work that we have to muster up, these are the characteristics of the Holy Spirit that are already in us. He will produce them as fruit when we willingly follow His way.

Jesus said, "All who love me will do what I say. My Father will love them, and we will come and make our home with each of them. Anyone who doesn't love me will not obey me. And remember, my words are not my own. What I am telling you is from the Father who sent me" (John 14:23–24). The Spirit of God gives us the desire to want to obey and enables us to do it. As He works His characteristics in us, He becomes our strength—the One who helps us obey, not from a heart of Law, but from real Love.

When we don't know what to pray, the Holy Spirit will help us there too. We don't always know the details about what we're praying for, but God does. Sometimes it's hard to hope without seeing the end, but God sees. So, we lean on His Spirit and follow His lead. The Apostle Paul explains, "We are weak and do not know how to pray, so the Spirit steps in and articulates prayers for us with groaning too profound for words. Don't you know that He who pursues and explores the human heart intimately knows the Spirit's mind because He pleads to God for His saints to align their lives with the will of God?" (Rom. 8:26–27 THE VOICE). When we lean into His leading, the Spirit of God will inspire us with the words to pray. He'll give us a heart of compassion and hope, and the strength we need to never give up. All that He does derives from the heart of God. What a gift the Holy Spirit truly is.

One of my first encounters with the Holy Spirit happened as a little girl, one Sunday at the end of church, when I heard the offer and call to be filled with the Holy Spirit. I was already saved,

I believed in Jesus, and I wanted all that God wanted to give. A flame was already burning in my heart, yet I desired to welcome more. With the faith of a child, I stepped down from my chair and walked to the altar for prayer. Kindly, a woman knelt beside me and helped me to welcome the filling and leading of God's Spirit. Although I was very young, I can still remember the moment—the peace and joy that filled my heart, and the smile that filled my face! I sensed the Lord's presence there and began to utter a unique sound. I felt a little shy, but the woman beside me reassured me that this was the start of my prayer language, a sign of the Holy Spirit.

Does this sound strange? I concur that it is! But we find such an example in Acts 2:4, where Luke recorded what happened in the Upper Room at Pentecost. Jesus had told His followers, "Do not leave Jerusalem until the Father sends you the gift he promised, as I told you before. John baptized with water, but in just a few days *you will be baptized with the Holy Spirit*" (Acts 1:4–5). So they were praying and waiting for the Promise when the Holy Spirit came. Luke wrote, "And everyone present was filled with the Holy Spirit and began speaking in other languages, as the Holy Spirit gave them this ability" (Acts 2:4). They were saved before Pentecost, but on that day, they welcomed an empowering baptism of the Holy Spirit.

What happened from there is recorded in the book of Acts— three thousand people believed in Jesus Christ and that was the start of the Church! A community that looked like family was formed. Here's the picture: "All the believers devoted themselves to the apostles' teaching, and to fellowship, and to sharing in meals (including the Lord's Supper), and to prayer" (Acts 2:42). And many miracles followed. Do you see the empowerment the Holy Spirit brings?

The story continues and we find another example in Acts 10:44-48 where the Lord sent Peter to tell the Gentiles about Jesus. Paul recalled the story, "Even as Peter was saying these things, the Holy Spirit fell upon all who were listening to the message. The Jewish believers who came with Peter were amazed that the gift of the Holy Spirit had been poured out on the Gentiles, too. For they heard them speaking in other tongues and praising God" (vv. 44–46). Speaking in unknown tongues looks to be a response to the gift of receiving the outpouring of the Holy Spirit.

It's another baptism—one that empowers all who will receive. Just like the disciples in Acts chapter 1, when we welcome the ongoing baptism and infilling of the Holy Spirit, we too receive more of His power. It's *His* power that enables us to know the heart of the Lord and to pray and believe for the impossible. It's the Holy Spirit's power that enables us to love and be loved and live for the Lord.

The prayer language that comes with welcoming the Holy Spirit produces great rewards. Jude, the brother of Jesus said, "But you, beloved, build yourselves up in your most holy faith. Pray in the Holy Spirit. Keep yourselves in the love of God while you are waiting for the mercy of our Lord Jesus Christ, which leads to eternal life" (Jude 1:20–21 MEV). By praying in the Holy Spirit we're allowing our spirit to commune directly with God's. We're enjoying intimacy with the Lord and delighting in His presence, so our spirit naturally responds to His. To pray with the Spirit is to strengthen our faith and to build up our spirit-man within. In close connection and communion with God, we are being prepared and equipped to take the joy of Jesus into the world!

Paul taught, "For he who speaks in an unknown tongue does not speak to men, but to God. For no one understands him, although in the spirit, he speaks mysteries" (1 Cor. 14:2 MEV). Verse 4 continues, "He who speaks in an unknown tongue edifies himself, but he who prophesies edifies the church." Paul concludes, "Well then, what shall I do? I will pray in the spirit, and I will also pray in words I understand. I will sing in the spirit, and I will also sing in words I understand" (1 Cor. 14:15).

Practically, when we first begin to speak in tongues, it might seem strange. It might seem like it's made up. It's normal to question, but as we continue to put our faith in believing God's Word, then great things can come to pass.

We don't have to understand the sounds, we just need to be willing to act in faith and trust the Giver of the gift. As we simply agree with the Spirit and give voice to our belief, our prayer language will grow into exactly what it's meant to be. When I was little, I practiced the new word throughout the day, and more sounds came. I enjoyed the closeness I felt when communing with the Lord in this special language of prayer. There were years I abandoned the practice, but as I returned to the Lord I found the gift was still available. Now, I pray in the Spirit and even sing in the Spirit to commune with and praise the Lord. Whether we're praying to praise or praying for breakthrough, we can use our language of prayer and trust that the Father is pleased.

Because we don't want to cause fear or confusion, we want to be mindful of others when praying in our spirit language. Paul taught, "I thank God that I speak in tongues more than any of you. But in a church meeting I would rather speak five understandable words to help others than ten thousand words in an unknown language" (1 Cor. 14:18–19).

At the very beginning of 1 Corinthians 14, Paul laid the foundation that love is to always be our highest goal. We can pray on our own and with other believers who share in the gift, and we can also tell others about the Promise that Jesus' disciples waited for and how many lives were changed after they received. We all need the powerful promise of the Holy Spirit with the sign of speaking in unknown tongues.

One of my favorite joys of being led by the Spirit is experiencing adventures with Him! Paul's words can help to excite and explain, "This is why the Scriptures say: Things never discovered or heard of before, things beyond our ability to imagine—these are the many things God has in store for all his lovers. But God now unveils these profound realities to us by the Spirit. Yes, he has revealed to us his inmost heart and deepest mysteries through the Holy Spirit, who constantly explores all things. After all, who can really see into a person's heart and know his hidden impulses except for that person's spirit? So it is with God. His thoughts and secrets are only fully understood by his Spirit, the Spirit of God" (1 Cor. 2:9–11 TPT).

The Spirit of God leads us into incredible possibilities. With Him, the future really is wide open! He inspires us with bravery and boldness to live what we believe and fulfill our calling. Without Him, I would have never dreamt of writing this book! I would have stayed held back by fear, holding on to what was comfortable, too insecure to trust the leading of the Holy Spirit. But our Father has good plans for us and His Spirit knows what they are! When we let Him lead, we can be transformed into a new creation, equipped and built up by His hand. Letting Him lead allows His incredible dreams for us to come true.

The Holy Spirit is our greatest helper for living a life that honors the Lord, purposefully hosts His presence, and impacts the world. His characteristics and gifts are available to *all* the followers of Jesus. He comes at Salvation and stays—to counsel, comfort, and embolden all who will listen for His voice and welcome His leading. He's the One who helps us live out the new life that we've been given. Let's respond in childlike faith and joyfully

> *It is by the Spirit that we allow the things of the flesh to be buried once and for all. And it is by the Spirit that we really learn to live!*

welcome the baptism of the Holy Spirit and enjoy the fulness of all that He brings. Paul taught, "For if you live according to the flesh, you will die, but if through the Spirit you put to death the deeds of the body, you will live. For as many as are led by the Spirit of God, these are the sons of God" (Rom. 8:13–14 MEV). It is *by the Spirit* that we allow the things of the flesh to be buried once and for all. And it is *by the Spirit* that we really learn to live!

Meditate

When did you first experience the Holy Spirit?

Have you welcomed the Spirit of God to be the Leader of your life? If not, ask the Lord to reveal what's holding you back.

Would you like more of the power of God to be evident in your life? If you'd like to be baptized in the Holy Spirit and receive the gift of praying in intimacy and power, with other tongues, begin to ask and welcome the gift. You can also join with another believer who's been baptized in the Holy Spirit and seek the Lord together.

Prayer

Father,

Thank You for giving me the Holy Spirit when I said "yes" to You. Holy Spirit, lead me and make me like Jesus.

Thank you for helping me to pray.

I welcome Your baptism and the gift of speaking in other tongues. Take me on adventures and help me to shine for You, fulfilling every dream that You have for me.

In Jesus' name, amen.

SECTION 4:
THE ROBE
A New Life

The wall was finished on the twenty-fifth day of the
month of Elul, in fifty-two days. When our enemies
heard it and all the surrounding nations saw it,
they were tremendously humbled. They perceived
that, because of our God, this work had been
accomplished.

—NEHEMIAH 6:15-16 MEV

THE LAST GIFT, THE new white robe shown in my vision, holds much meaning. It represents our new identity in Christ Jesus. In Him we are royal sons and daughters of the Living God. No longer broken, insecure, and oppressed, we now know that we're a chosen people meant to thrive under His hand. We are growing up in our Father's kingdom, taking our place, and becoming mature and strong. We're growing in trust for the Lord, abiding in Him, and we believe that we're alive for a purpose.

The Father has made us to give Him glory by shining like a bride made beautiful for her groom. Readying for the return of our King, we will put on the righteousness of Jesus and wear our new identity in Him.

Isaiah said it beautifully,

> I am overwhelmed with joy in the Lord my God! For he has dressed me with the clothing of salvation and draped me in a robe of righteousness. I am like a bridegroom dressed for his wedding or a bride with her jewels. The Sovereign Lord will show his justice to the nations of the world. Everyone will praise him! His righteousness will be like a garden in early spring, with plants springing up everywhere.
>
> —ISAIAH 61:10

Our new life declares our restoration and gets the attention of the hurting, the lonely, the lost. They need what we have, and we are ready to give!

To live and to give what we've received, let's continue becoming our Father's design as we abide with the One who gives us all that we need. Let's honor Him—King Jesus—with our living and reflect Him rightly. As we wear His righteousness, we will impact the world around us for Him!

Chapter Seventeen

Living Loved

And they were all singing this new song of praise
to the Lamb: "Because you were slaughtered for us,
you are worthy to take the scroll and open its seals.
Your blood was the price paid to redeem us. You
purchased us to bring us to God out of every tribe,
language, people group, and nation. You have chosen
us to serve our God and formed us into a kingdom of
priests who reign on the earth."

—REVELATION 5:9–10 TPT

WE ARE DEARLY LOVED by our incredible Creator God. Jesus has already proved it. Living loved is *receiving* His forgiveness, acceptance, sonship, delight, and every good gift that the Father, Son, and Holy Spirit has to give. Living loved is putting on the priceless robe of righteousness Jesus has provided. It's being aware of His covering, receiving the wisdom of His Word, and enjoying the empowering presence of the Holy Spirit. Will we put on what we've been given? Will we wear what we need? Will we reach out and receive the gift of being so loved?

Receiving isn't always easy. It doesn't always come naturally. But all we have to do is keep believing and trust in the One who meets our every need. Like a beloved child reaching out both hands in expectation of a surprise gift, we believe that the Father is good and we take hold of the things that He gives. This is how we honor Him and live beloved.

The Lord knew from the very beginning that like all of humanity that's gone before us, we too would choose self-preservation, retaliation, rebellion, and pride. Our imperfections haven't taken Him by surprise. He knows us down to the very core, and still He says, *"Daughter, Son, yes, you! I choose you. I am yours, and you are Mine. We are family forever! Come out of hiding. Come out of shame. Come out of fear and trust in My name."*

> **It's time to believe that the Father really is as good as He says He is.**

We are His chosen children, made alive by His hands. He has chosen to make us His home! It's time to believe it. It's time to believe that the Father really is as good as He says He is. It's time to believe that we really are the way our Father sees us. We are loved right now, and we already are what we will one day become.

The Lord has called you by name. He has called us, each one, to come out of the dark and into the light. He has drawn us to Himself, into love. Love is who He is; it's not just something He does. He loves without conditions. He has remained faithful to His love for our entire lives. Because of our believing in the sacrificial life and love of Jesus, the Father has welcomed us with open arms. Being His beloved child is our identity! Now, we experience and know firsthand what it's like to be loved by Love Himself. What incredible joy! No one has ever loved us or will ever love us like this.

How does He love us? Let us count the ways....

Living loved by the Father feels like acceptance. Within His approval, we're given room for our immaturity and understanding during our growth. The Lord knows our humanity and great need for Him, and He allows us to be who we are and where we are, while we're learning to receive. He is so very patient with us and loves us by staying with us throughout our entire process of learning, practicing, and maturing into His way of living. He sees us as what we will one day become yet loves us just as we are today. He helps us learn to accept and love ourselves too. Remembering how He proved His love on a Cross, let's honor Him by believing that we are fully embraced as His child.

Unfortunately, we aren't very good at championing other people when we don't believe in our own worth, so we must believe it, not only for ourselves, but for others too. We must settle into who we truly are and make peace with the way we've been designed. That is living loved. Then, as we discover purpose and fulfillment, we can cheer on the people around us.

Instead of comparing ourselves to others and coming up short, and instead of feeling insecure in thoughts of jealousy, the Father wants us to appreciate who we are. Instead of looking at others and wanting what they have—desiring their talents, looks, relationships, money, position, or anything different from what we've been given—He wants us to be satisfied with how He designed us as His creation. He wants us to take our place in His heart and kingdom.

When teaching about the family of God, Paul explained that we're similar to a body with different parts fulfilling various needs, each one necessary to complete the body and function as a whole. He said, "The human body has many parts, but the many parts make up one whole body. So it is with the body of Christ." He continues, "But our bodies have many parts, and God has put each part just where he wants it" (1 Cor. 12:12, 18). We need to be at peace with who we are and take our special place because I need the real you and you need the authentic me.

If we're consumed with comparing ourselves to others or wishing that things in our lives were different—that we were different, then we won't appreciate who we were created to be. We'll miss the joy of discovering our uniqueness. We'll miss discovering and growing the gifts He's placed inside.

Comparison and jealousy are thieves of contentment and joy. Instead, our confidence can come from knowing that we are so very loved. As we believe it, we find security. We find that we were created for so much more.

> *Comparison and jealousy are thieves of contentment and joy.*

I know this to be true because I've struggled to believe I'm accepted and loved just as I am. Instead of believing in love, I've listened to the thieving thoughts of comparison and jealousy. It stems from insecurity and pride—two attributes that seem opposite, yet they are linked. Pride says I should have what I want, and insecurity agrees, hoping it will be the thing to bring value. Living in lack (believing I'm not enough) leaves me discouraged and wanting. It leaves me unsatisfied with the life I lead. But this doesn't honor the Lord, it demonstrates ungratefulness for the life He's given and inhibits me from enjoying and multiplying His love.

Just because someone has something we don't have (wealth, looks, position, or family) doesn't mean that we have any less value or anything less to give. Our worth is not depleted in any way. We are still wanted, still needed, and our value is still secure. We may not always receive accolades from others, but our Father is always watching, and what He cares about is the attitude of our hearts. If we'll choose contentment over comparison, then He'll be pleased every time. If we'll let His love in, then He will be honored.

When Paul taught about seeking God's acceptance he said, "Your identity before God has nothing to do with circumcision or uncircumcision. What really matters is following God's commandments. So everyone should continue to live faithful in the situation of life in which they were called to follow Jesus." He continues, "Since a great price was paid for your redemption, stop having the mind-set of a slave" (1 Cor. 7:19–20, 23 TPT).

To start thinking like a chosen, adopted child of God, we must embrace the truth of who we are and step into our new identity. Then we can discover what the Lord has called us to do. And we don't have to guess what that is, because the Father already knows. Recently, I was reading the familiar verse of Jeremiah 29:11, when I heard it in a whole new way. It says, "'For *I know* the plans I have for you,' says the Lord. 'They are plans for good and not for disaster, to give you a future and a hope'" (my emphasis). I heard the emphasis on God *knowing* what His plans are for you and me—"*For I know*." They are specific and unique.

They hold eternal meaning, bring great fulfillment, and extend the kingdom of God. And *He knows* what His plans are.

There's a specific calling on each one of our lives and everyone has an integral part to play. When we don't take the place that our Father has purposed for us and we don't discover what He's designed us to do, then our spot sits empty; our purpose is left undone.

As we find and take our place, we know security, purpose, and joy. So, we're more mindful to encourage others, who are discovering and becoming too. By securing ourselves within our own value and purpose, we resist jealousy and competition. We live at peace with ourselves and with one another as we enjoy the process of becoming more like Jesus, while finding the freedom to reflect Him through our unique personalities, abilities, and gifts.

The enemy doesn't want us to live as the beloved son or daughter that God designed us to be. He doesn't want us to fulfill the plans our Father has for us. He wants us to be distracted by discontentment and comparison, and he'll try anything to keep us from realizing and becoming who we truly are.

Living loved is taking our place at the Father's table and finding where we really belong. It's where we find our home. Taking our place is the way to finding what we've been looking for all of our lives. No longer disconnected by unbelief, we're secure in the Lord's love, which reaches our heart and binds us to His everlasting presence and delight.

There's no need to strive to earn this love, we simply abide in Him and receive it. This happens by spending one-on-one time with the Lord. Jesus said, "And everything I've taught you is so that the peace which is in me will be in you and will give you great confidence as you rest in me" (John 16:33 TPT). We've been created to live in this love. In the safe love of the Father is where we find our confidence. It's where we belong.

Living loved also leads us to finding freedom. Because we belong to Jesus (doesn't that feel good?), we are free people! We are freed from our mistakes, free to lean on His strength in our weakness, and instead of staying stuck in immaturity, we're free to grow. We are freed from worrying about the future and secured in the foundation of Christ—free from all fear. We are free to stop comparing and to live loved, fathered, and covered by the Perfect One.

Flourishing in the joy of being completely known, fully accepted, and delightfully loved, we're free to fly! We're free to become a beautiful life that honors our King.

This lifelong process is beautiful to the Father, and He enjoys watching, teaching, and skillfully sculpting us in every phase. Under His care, we transform into something that never was! Like a butterfly that was once an egg, then a caterpillar, and a chrysalis, over time we are becoming something new. What beauty we're becoming because of God's tender love. Let this truth sink in, "God of Heaven's Armies, you find so much beauty in your people! They're like lovely sanctuaries of your presence" (Psa. 84:1 TPT).

Tenderly loved, we are free to share who we really are and to give of ourselves, because we know that in the Father's house, there is always more than enough.

Our response to this love that we've been so generously given, is to return it and make it multiply. The more we know how good it feels to be unconditionally and boundlessly loved, the more we *have* to give what we've received!

To freely give and to fully enjoy the peace, contentment, and love the Father has for us, we want to go back to seeing like a child. Jesus said, "For the Kingdom of God belongs to those who are like these children. I tell you the truth, anyone who doesn't receive the Kingdom of God like a child will never enter it" (Mark 10:14–15).

Can you remember the fun and freedom of learning to roller skate, unafraid of trying something new? What about jumping in muddy puddles made from the water hose, or playing in the neighborhood with friends on a slow, golden afternoon? Remember those childhood days that were long and carefree, and the ability to be without fear for tomorrow—too fully present in the moment of the day to give worry any room? I hope you can recall the trust and freedom that came from being cared for and securely loved as a child. With eyes of wonder, the gift of a day was never wasted. Even the simplest things were appreciated and enjoyed to the full.

Our faithful Father wants us to return to that trusting, childlike way of experiencing life with Him. He wants us to appreciate being fathered and loved by Him so we can enjoy Him and His many gifts. God loves watching us celebrate the life we've been given by delighting in the things that He's made. Consider the wonder of creation, and the gift of relationships, provision, and life itself. All have been given by the Father. Where would we be without His kindness? The Lord has provided all that we need and so much more!

God has given good gifts and fashioned us with His own hands. He's breathed His breath into our lungs, and we are alive because we've been chosen to live! The Lord God decided if we would be male or female, chose where we'd be born, and specified into which family. The location of our birth and the places we call home are not by coincidence. Every event—the good ones as well as the ones that have caused us pain—hold purpose. God is in every one of our details working things out for His glory and our good. We want to fulfill His plans! We want to take our place at His table.

As chosen ones who are dearly loved, will we come alive to who we truly are? Will we find pleasure in the people around us as they're becoming too? Will we fit together in the family and so fulfill the purpose of the church to ready the world for the return of our King? Will we dare to believe and step into our purpose? Will we dare to champion others in theirs?

Like a child, let's enjoy the security and delight of living in our Father's love. Let's keep becoming and cheer others on to do the same. Let's open our arms and receive all that our Father, Jesus, and the Spirit of God has to give.

Meditate

Find a quiet place and set your mind on the Father. He wants to demonstrate His love to you. Relish the experience of being loved by Love Himself. Linger there.

What message do you see, sense, or hear? Follow it to find what the Father is saying.

Prayer

Father,

You truly have loved me with an everlasting love. A thousand thank-yous would never be enough. I'm so grateful, and I receive Your love.

I am secure in Your love, and I will always have a place.

Thank You for accepting me as I am, while seeing me as what I will become. You are the Potter, and I am the clay; transform me into Your design.

Your love is the best love. I receive it. I believe it. And I live in it, like a joyful, grateful, and trusting child. I will share it and make it multiply!

Thank You for loving me like You do.

I love You too.

In Jesus' name, amen.

Chapter Eighteen

Love without Limits

**My little children, don't just talk about love as an idea
or a theory. Make it your true way of life, and live in
the pattern of gracious love.**

— 1 JOHN 3:18 THE VOICE

EXPERIENCING THE UNCONDITIONAL LOVE of the
Father firsthand changes everything. Before we knew His
love, we didn't desire the mercy of the Father, so we had no mercy to give. We didn't realize the great gift of salvation or know of
our need. But now we know. We know Love Himself and we've
received His love and mercy, so now we have it to give! God
has chosen us to be His expression to one another on the earth.
Overflowing with His love, we're starting to really notice one
another. We're beginning to notice and care for one another's
needs. We're really learning to love!

God's love changes us and the filters through which we look
at the world. We're learning to see through the eyes of understanding and connection rather than offense, judgment, or distance. Every one of us longs to be loved. We want to be accepted
and to belong. These needs are first and foremost met by the
Father, but we can support and strengthen one another by loving
unconditionally, side by side, like the Lord loves us.

Love-without-limits love doesn't just happen—we have to first be known and loved by the perfect parent, our Father God. Clothed by Him, we can forsake our old, self-preserving ways. We're able to learn to put others first and to keep on giving even when we don't feel like it. We're able to learn to love independent from our circumstances, freed from our old habits and from how we feel. Learning to love from our own acceptance enables us to make, keep, and protect our connections with others, even when it's hard. This kind of love requires leaning on, listening to, and allowing the Lord to lead.

We've all been designed by our Creator so uniquely, and our upbringings and experiences can vary widely. Personalities, too, can be so different that it's sometimes hard to relate to one another and achieve connection. But we want to *find* common ground and *make* connections with the people the Lord has put into our lives. To grow in understanding, we'll have to seek it out. We'll need to be open to listening to other perspectives and willing to be open with our own lives too.

I love personality tests, especially the Enneagram, because they explain our motivations and how we see the world. They help us better understand why we all do the things we do. Understanding then leads to compassion, and compassion leads to patience while we're learning and growing. It helps us resist offense and take things less personally.

On the Enneagram, my husband John is a 1, called *the Reformer*. He sees what needs to be made right in the world and gets right to work. I'm a 4, *the Romantic*, so I'm more of a feeler than a do-er. And there's the rub! We're learning to appreciate our differences and value how we complement one another. Seeking to understand has added a rich depth of dimension to our relationship. It's brought about a greater love.

Investigating how friends and family receive and actually feel loved is another valuable tool for loving unconditionally. *The Five Love Languages* by Gary Chapman is a classic but relevant resource that helps us love well. When we take the time to learn about the people around us, it shows we respect who they are and value their uniqueness.

Often, we assume others hear the same narrative about the world that we do, or we think they feel loved the same way, but that's not always the case. Listening with understanding demonstrates that we hear and appreciate their

> *Loving others as they are and in their own unique language makes way for the love to get in.*

perspective. It demonstrates love. Loving others as they are and in their own unique language makes way for the love to get in.

What about relationships that challenge our love rather than receive it?

There are times when people choose separation over connection. Sometimes they even choose to manipulate. It can be difficult to determine how to love unconditionally when we experience their rejection or attempt at unhealthy control. What a gift to have God's Word so available for finding wisdom. Aren't we thankful to have the Spirit of God residing within? He will show us how to follow the heart of the Father when trust has been broken, and when we've been hurt. The Holy Spirit will help us navigate the workings of our heart, to cooperate and change where we need to, while praying for the other person. When needed, He'll help us create healthy boundaries, not out of fear or retaliation, but with a humble heart and wisdom.

A dear mentor taught me that a boundary is not like a high stone wall with signage that says, "Keep out!" A healthy boundary looks more like a picket fence between two houses. Both neighbors can come to visit at the fence, if and when they choose. But they don't barge into one another's homes and come crashing through the front door. They don't force or manipulate. They honor and respect. To envision this kind of boundary will help us set healthy expectations and stick to them. When challenges come knocking, we can continue to stand for what's right, while looking for the best in others and praying for restoration.

We've all experienced disappointments, broken trust, and painful rejection from people we hold dear. This kind of pain can feel like a direct hit. Often, it pierces so deeply that it seems safer to keep it inside rather than facing the truth.

Wounded by such a hit, and now down the road a ways, I can now see that it offers opportunity to really learn to love. It gives us a chance to reject pride, to grow, and to love, even when it hurts.

What do we do when these painful feelings are entwined with family or others that we're in ongoing relationships with? What do we do when people are hard to love?

We keep on telling the truth. We're honest with what we're feeling, and we experience the hurt. Then we separate the actions of others from our love for them and we walk out forgiveness and patience with the help of the Holy Spirit. If we need to make amends, then we take time to pray and prepare, and say what needs to be said. We listen. We give space where space is needed. Along the way, we stand in our convictions and place healthy boundaries, while also keeping our heart pure before the Lord.

As we practice, our ability to love is steadied as we rely on the Lord. Rather than relying on our feelings or our own strength, we stand on truth and act from the love we've received. In obedience, our patience grows stronger and more constant until it truly becomes a part of who we are. In time, the strength of the Lord will become our own and we'll be able to love, in spite of what we see or feel.

When the rocky relationship is with one of our children, it's vital that our love for them stays steady and dependable. As parents, we're their first source and example of the Father's love and it's a precious opportunity that we don't want to miss. We want to be a place of safety, acceptance, and hope. It is never too late to begin to love this way. I know this to be true.

As connection is restored, then love can flow and be welcomed and received. This love brings healing and acceptance to our child's wounded heart, and with time and consistency, their heart will respond.

Sometimes the intensity of our love clouds our judgment and fear steers us into trying to control their decisions. When we do that, we place faith in ourselves to bring change instead of praying and trusting in God. So often, we want to protect the ones we love from experiencing the pain of their choices, but the

Father doesn't keep us from hard things. In fact, He allows us to experience them so we can grow.

Discomfort is often a part of the process of gaining new understanding, growing in maturity, and receiving new life where death once was. If we choose to "save" others from feeling the consequence of their choices, we'll just delay their opportunity to learn and grow from their mistakes. Instead, we can trust in God and show our love by being a safe place and staying available as they navigate the challenges of life.

Unconditional love doesn't try to control others; it actually sets people free. It can be very frightening to let go and let God,

> *Unconditional love doesn't try to control others; it actually sets people free.*

so we must keep our mind protected through prayer, community with encouraging believers, and through the Word. With so many complex situations, we want to stay close to the Lord and continue to seek Him for wisdom and guidance. He is the One who's working things out for our good and for the good of those we love.

If we remain mindful of the many challenges of the maturing process that we're all going through in this turbulent world, it will help our hearts stay soft, quick to forgive, and steady to love. True love *seeks* to understand. It *looks* for common ground. True love works to maintain connection, yet never forces itself. It allows room for others to be who they are and where they are, while always hoping for good. We find this in 1 Corinthians 13:4–7 (TPT):

Love is large and incredibly patient. Love is gentle and consistently kind to all. It refuses to be jealous when blessing comes to someone else. Love does not brag about one's achievements nor inflate its own importance. Love does not traffic in shame and disrespect, nor selfishly seek its own honor. Love is not easily irritated or quick to take offense. Love joyfully celebrates honesty and finds no delight in what is wrong. Love is a safe place of shelter, for it never stops believing the best for others. Love never takes failure as defeat, for it never gives up.

Consider, again, how completely the Lord loves us, even in our unfinished state. This truth motivates us to live out true love.

It's this kind of love that we want to give to fellow believers. After all, we're supposed to be so good at loving one another, that we're known for it! (see John 13:34-35). We should look and act differently than the self-serving norm of the world. Our love for one another should be so extravagant that it attracts the attention of people who don't know the Savior yet.

Loving unconditionally shines a light for all the world to see. Extending acceptance, making room, and looking for the priceless treasures that God has placed inside every one of His children extends that light. We love by becoming a safe place for honesty, healing, and growth. We know how incredible it feels to transform and grow into something new, so we can love by encouraging others to become their true self, too. Celebrating our differences and championing one another will make us known for the way we love. The lost will be attracted to the light of our love and the church will grow into a strong and mature house for the presence of the Lord. Through our love, Jesus will be magnified!

We have opportunity after opportunity to be a beautiful reflection of the King by choosing connection and choosing to love. Our highest goal of loving one another without limits is to bring glory to the Father. Let's reflect Him well by meditating on and living out His way of love. John said, "Our love for others is our grateful response to the love God first demonstrated to us. Anyone can say, 'I love God,' yet have hatred toward another believer. This makes him a phony, because if you don't love a brother or sister, whom you can see, how can you truly love God, whom you can't see?" (1 John 4:19–20 TPT). We do love Him, and we are ready to show it!

Meditation

Is the Holy Spirit bringing to mind anyone that you need to return to loving? Is there a relationship in which you've withheld your love?

Ask the Lord to show you any areas where you can better love without limits. Do you need to let the Lord's love into that place? Listen and follow His leading.

Prayer

Father,

Thank You for showing me what love without limits really looks like. I love being loved by You.

Through relationships, You're stretching and growing me to become more like You. I want to love the people around me well and I need Your help. Help me accept others as they are and value our differences. Help me to see people the way You do, so I can help them shine and take their place in the Body.

In the relationships that challenge or reject my love, help me humble myself and love anyway. Thank You for Your wisdom. Help me to set healthy boundaries where they need to be.

Help me to love with an everlasting, no-limits kind of love. My love is a light for You!

In Jesus' name, amen.

Chapter Nineteen

Discovering Your Gifts

**For You shaped me, inside and out. You knitted me
together in my mother's womb long before I took my
first breath. I will offer You my grateful heart, for I
am Your unique creation, filled with wonder and awe.
You have approached even the smallest details with
excellence; Your works are wonderful; I carry this
knowledge deep within my soul.**

—PSALM 139:13–14 THE VOICE

THE LORD GOD FORMED you and me with His very
own hands. There has never been a moment when His
eyes weren't on His creation. Imagine Him imagining you while
penning plans of purpose and delight. To fulfill His dreams, He's
made us uniquely, with abilities that hold eternal purpose. He's
given us gifts to reflect His glory and to expand His kingdom on
the earth.

But before our Creator asks us to do anything with Him or
for Him, He wants to first settle His love for us deep into our
souls. He wants us to first know Him and be known by Him.
That's the ground we've been covering thus far, as we've found
His love for us through His faithfulness, through our restoration and healing. We know now that He's with us and we know

how to spend our days fellowshipping with Him. Walking with Him has brought an added delight, because the more we discover who our Father God truly is, the more we're uncovering who we are. Romans 12:3 says it well: "The only accurate way to understand ourselves is by what God is and by what he does for us, not by what we are and what we do for him" (THE MESSAGE).

Our Creator knows exactly who we are. He knows the unique ways He's made us to reflect Him and the ways we'll find fulfillment as we're discovering ourselves and the gifts He's planted within. Paul explained, "For we are the product of His hand, *heaven's poetry etched on lives*, created in the Anointed, Jesus, to accomplish the good works God arranged long ago" (Eph. 2:10 THE VOICE).

What has He arranged and written about you? What is the purpose of your design? And where do you fit into the body of Christ? To discover the answers, we look for the gifts within. When teaching the church of Corinth about gifts that the Holy Spirit gives, Paul said:

> **What has He arranged and written about you?**

A spiritual gift is given to each of us so we can help each other. To one person the Spirit gives the ability to give wise advice; to another the same Spirit gives a message of special knowledge. The same Spirit gives great faith to another, and to someone else the one Spirit gives the gift of healing. He gives one person the power to perform miracles, and another the ability to prophesy. He gives someone else the ability to discern whether a message is from the Spirit of

God or from another spirit. Still another person is given the ability to speak in unknown languages, while another is given the ability to interpret what is being said.

—1 CORINTHIANS 12:7–10

In the body of Christ there are many differing parts function-ing uniquely for the good and health of the whole. To take our place and fulfill our position is to be a part of something greater than ourselves. It's to exist and function in the kingdom family, the family that is forever!

To build up that family, Jesus gives gifts to the church. Paul continued, "Now these are the gifts Christ gave to the church: the apostles, the prophets, the evangelists, and the pastors and teach-ers. Their responsibility is to equip God's people to do his work and build up the church, the body of Christ" (Eph. 4:11–12). Even those who occupy the positions we hold high are there to strengthen and mature the church. They're not there to do all the work. The apostles, prophets, evangelists, pastors and teachers are there to equip us to do our part in the work. It's time to ma-ture by feeding ourselves daily and taking our place. It's time to appreciate every position in the body and to function as a whole.

The Apostle Peter tells us of some of the gifts, "God has given each of you a gift from his great variety of spiritual gifts. Use them well to serve one another. Do you have the gift of speak-ing? Then speak as though God himself were speaking through you. Do you have the gift of helping others? Do it with all the strength and energy that God supplies. Then everything you do will bring glory to God through Jesus Christ" (1 Pet. 4:10–11).

What a bounty! There are so many ways to give God glory and there's so much more to learn about spiritual gifts, but at the heart of it all is the joy of discovering who the Father made us to be and growing up to take our place in the family of God. We get to be a part of encouraging, strengthening, and building up His beautiful church, to help make her ready for the return of Christ our King!

We want to be that built up, mature bride of Christ. We want to take our place and fulfill the Father's desire. We want Him to be pleased and we want to be a part of the song that will be heard from around the throne of God. Imagine the vision that God gave to John:

> Then I heard again what sounded like the shout of a vast crowd or the roar of mighty ocean waves or the crash of loud thunder: "Praise the Lord! For the Lord our God, the Almighty, reigns. Let us be glad and rejoice, and let us give honor to him. For the time has come for the wedding feast of the Lamb, and his bride has prepared herself. She has been given the finest of pure white linen to wear." For the fine linen represents the good deeds of God's holy people.
>
> —REVELATION 19:6–8

How do we wear a white robe? We realize our position, discover our gifts, and use them to serve the Lord and His body. Think about your natural ability and the areas of creating, serving, or leading that make you come alive. Where do you thrive and find fulfillment? Your place of gifting will not be without challenge or work, but it will energize and see you through, to get tough jobs done. It might be helpful to try serving in different ways—within the church and without, to discover where you fit in.

Discovering our gifts gives God glory by becoming who He's made us to be and fulfilling our potential and design. To be satisfied with the way God made us and to serve faithfully in the place that He's planted us is all part of our discovery. While we grow, we continue to seek the Lord and spend time with Him in His Word and Spirit, and we listen as He tells us who we are. Taking our place and doing what He's designed us to do is how the Lord expands His kingdom and fulfills His plans upon the earth. What a joy and a responsibility it is to partner with the Lord!

John and I discovered that we enjoy practicing the gift of hospitality. It's one that Scripture tells us all to grow in! Paul taught, "When God's people are in need, be ready to help them. Always be eager to practice hospitality" (Rom. 12:13). John and I enjoy having people over and serving them. We like to create a peaceful setting where friends feel welcome and secure. We make a place for people to be real and look for ways to encourage and strengthen each one who visits our home. It's a place to pray, to cry and to laugh, and to extend peace, hope, and love.

Whatever our gifting is, we want to humbly, yet confidently function in it. Instead of comparing our position or gift to another's, we want to grow and become who *we* were made to be. That way, the Body of Christ is in alignment, and we're not trying to function outside of our design. We're taking our place, and that place is just right, fulfilling, and pleasing to the Lord.

First Corinthians 12 reminds us that we are all important. Every single of one us is valued and included in fulfilling God's plans. My place in the body of Christ and my gifts that allow me to serve Him there are no more important or less important than yours. Being who God made us to be, taking our place, and functioning well in our gifting are more ways to love one another. Paul taught, "Don't just pretend to love others. Really love them. Hate what is wrong. Hold tightly to what is good. Love each other with genuine affection, and take delight in honoring each other" (Rom. 12:9–10). Not only do we want to have peace with our position, we also want to honor the place that God has given others. It's another way to wear His righteousness and display our love.

If we will keep trusting the Lord and follow His leading with faith, He'll continue to show us the way. He will show us our gifts and help us develop and use them. And along the way, His dreams for us naturally unfold as His plans are carried out. This isn't a striving or a working to earn our Father's love, but an enjoyable discovery of who He made us to be! We are always learning and growing. Aren't we thankful the Father doesn't require perfection to serve and partner with Him?

We can trust the Lord to continue to unfold who we are, and to fulfill every plan He's purposed for us as we seek and listen, and trust and obey, each step of the way. He will provide all we need to fulfill the dreams He's planned and penned for you and me. We just stay close and follow Him with wonder, while becoming and fulfilling who He's made us to be—all for His glory!

Meditate

What gifts has God given you and where do your passions lie? How can you utilize what God's given to serve the church and to bring Him glory?

Read and meditate on 1 Corinthians 12 and Romans 12. What do you hear the Lord saying about using the gifts He's placed within?

Prayer

Father,

Thank You for creating me uniquely. Thank You for knowing me so well. Help me to keep growing into Your design. Show me the gifts You've given me so I can love and honor You by serving Your bride. I want to mature and to take my place. I desire all that You have to give for building up the church.

I love You, Lord.

In Jesus' name, amen.

Chapter Twenty

Give It Away

Now, if anyone is enfolded into Christ, he has become an entirely new creation. All that is related to the old order has vanished. Behold, everything is fresh and new.

And God has made all things new, and reconciled us to himself, and given us the ministry of reconciling others to God.

—2 CORINTHIANS 5:17–18 TPT

WHAT A JOURNEY OF restoration we've taken together! Remembering the vision that started it all takes us back to the broken-down wall. Remember relating to the people in the beginning of the Book of Nehemiah, the ones who lived in unrest, inhibited by fear, unable to freely enjoy the life God had given? Remember their shame and how they were hindered from glorifying God with their lives? But remember too, the Lord didn't leave them there! He sent Nehemiah, whose heart was broken for their oppression. He fulfilled God's work by serving the people whom his heart hurt for. God blessed the work by providing all they needed for rebuilding the wall and setting a strong foundation. Nehemiah brought the people vision and encouraged them with the message that restoration was coming!

Each family worked together to rebuild and defend their homes. Each one had a part and found hope in the process of restoration. Surrounded by security, they could live as the chosen children of God! With the wall in place, so much was restored. Once again, the people knew safety. They gathered together again at the Temple, where the Law of God was read and where they were deeply moved. They worshiped with thanksgiving, remembering where they had once been. Awakened by the love of the Lord, they discovered their identity and found their purpose. Fulfilling God's plan to love, honor, and serve Him, they took their place and worshiped with their lives.

> *In the eyes of Jesus, we have finally found acceptance, we have discovered His peace. This is a whole new life!*

It was all the Lord's doing. He chose them, each one. He had a plan and a purpose to be carried out through His children. God put it on Nehemiah's heart to rebuild the wall to secure His people so they could become who He designed them to be. The Lord wanted their restoration and He brought it about through men and women who were willing to work with Him.

We, too, once lived like those people in insecurity. So tired of living exposed to the arrows of darkness, and weary of making our own way, we realized we needed a strong, safe place to dwell. Finally willing to submit to Jesus as LORD, to abide in Him, and to yield to His Lordship completely, we gave God control.

Now entering the *fullness* of our salvation, love has surrounded us like we've never known. In the eyes of Jesus, we have finally found acceptance; we have discovered His peace. This is a whole new life! Set free to know our Maker and to trust in Him, there's so much to celebrate! We're finding who we really are and discovering what we're made to do! Transformed and empowered to be bold, we're fulfilled by the purpose of God's good plans. We're becoming something so much more than we were outside of His sheltering presence. Now it's our joy to give *Him* control, to follow *His* lead, and give honor to *His* name! It is our joy to be a dwelling place for God!

So how do we continue becoming all that God wants us to be? How do we fulfill all the good plans He has for us? We keep our eyes on Jesus and continue to abide and trust in Him. The inspiration for the title of this book is found in 1 Peter 2:4-5. It is our key: "So keep coming to him who is the Living Stone—though he was rejected and discarded by men but chosen by God and is priceless in God's sight. Come and be his 'living stones' who are continually being assembled into a sanctuary for God. For now you serve as holy priests, offering up spiritual sacrifices that he readily accepts through Jesus Christ" (TPT).

To keep becoming a house for the Lord and to multiply and give away the love and restoration we've received, we remember that Jesus is our One thing. He made the way for us to be welcomed into the Father's family. Our primary purpose is to love Him in return and to remember the price He paid for the depth of love He has for us. Jesus will forever reign as Lord over our heart, mind, and will, because *He keeps His promises*. No one can remove us from His hand (see John 10:28-29).

The Lord God will continue shaping us into His design as we abide in Him! Let's join Paul in believing, "I am confident that the Creator, who has begun such a great work among you, will not stop in *mid-design* but *will* keep perfecting you until the day Jesus the Anointed, our *Liberating King, returns to redeem the world*" (Phil. 1:6 THE VOICE).

Through our ongoing healing, restoration, and testing, and through our continual surrender to Truth Himself, we are becoming living stones. We are becoming our truest selves and a living house for our beautiful King!

Not everyone will understand our new life. Some will be uncomfortable with the new confidence, joy, and freedom that we carry. They may need time to understand. Others just won't get it; they won't appreciate who we're becoming or support the purpose we're called to fulfill. That's okay. Jesus knows just how it feels. He was able to withstand being misunderstood and mistreated because He valued the voice of His Father. It was unto Him, not man, that Jesus lived to please.

Look at this example written in Mark, "Since it was the Sabbath, Jesus' enemies watched him closely. If he healed the man's hand, they planned to accuse him of working on the Sabbath. Jesus said to the man with the deformed hand, 'Come and stand in front of everyone'" (3:2–3).

Jesus didn't hide or heal him in the back of the room, He obeyed the Father for all to see—not prideful, but connected, trusting, and obedient. The story continues, "Then he turned to his critics and asked, 'Does the law permit good deeds on the Sabbath, or is it a day for doing evil? Is this a day to save life or to destroy it?' But they wouldn't answer him. He looked around at them angrily and was deeply saddened by their hard hearts. Then he said to the man, 'Hold out your hand.' So the man held out his hand, and it was restored!" (vv. 4–5). Our God is always about restoration—He is always saying, *"This is a day to save a life!"* And He works through us when we humbly, yet courageously walk in our identity and fulfill our calling.

The way we live out our calling is unique, but we all carry the same message of reconciliation:

> **We are ambassadors of the Anointed One who carry the message of Christ to the world, as though God were tenderly pleading with them directly through our lips. So we tenderly plead with you on Christ's behalf, "Turn back to God and be reconciled to him." For God made the only one who did not know sin to become sin for us, so that we might become the righteousness of God through our union with him.**
>
> —2 CORINTHIANS 5:20–21 TPT

When misunderstanding or persecution comes, we must not stop. We must continue becoming the daughter or son that God says we are and continue carrying out the plans He's written for us to fulfill. We must give the message of life!

Finding strength in the believers beside us, let's take our unique place as a piece of the church, and stay committed to the body. Instead of seeing through the lens of isolation, strife, jealousy, or competition (which are all rooted in fear), we remember that our place is secure in the Father. We honor others and respect their positions too. Remembering that we're unique individuals with various shapes of personality, equipped with special gifts, strengths, and even weaknesses, each one of us is vitally needed and leaves a hole when we don't take our place and do our part. So, we champion the people in our lives and are good at cheering one another on! As long as it's up to us, we choose to live in peace, remembering Paul's encouragement, "Do all that you can to live in peace with everyone" (Rom. 12:18).

In living and breathing relationships, we aren't afraid of the imperfections or immaturity others temporarily hold. We understand that we're all being perfected, and we *continue* to walk beside one another as we resist offense. As faithful friends, we stick around, even when it gets tough. The Father is faithful too, and always provides the strength we need to follow His way and become His mature and beautiful bride. Let this truth go deep: "But you are God's chosen treasure—priests who are kings, a spiritual 'nation' set apart as God's devoted ones. He called you out of darkness to experience his marvelous light, and now he claims you as his very own. He did this so that you would broadcast his glorious wonders *throughout the world*" (1 Pet. 2:9 TPT).

Consider the words of C. S. Lewis from *The Weight of Glory*, "There are no *ordinary* people. You have never talked to a mere mortal...it is immortals whom we joke with, work with, marry, snub, and exploit—immortal horrors or everlasting splendours" (46). These are the ones beside us, the sons and daughters of our Father's design who carry His image too.

Remembering how we've been restored, our hearts break for the hurting, and like Nehemiah, we're inspired to share the message of restoration. With hearts on fire, we burn to tell of what God has done.

Many are still living outside of the shelter of Jesus and haven't come into His rest. They need to be restored. They must have the message we carry.

Just before ascending into heaven, Jesus said, "Go into all the world and preach the Good News to everyone. Anyone who believes and is baptized will be saved. But anyone who refuses to believe will be condemned" (Mark 16:15–16). We've experienced firsthand this good news and we know the joy that it brings!

The prophet Isaiah described a beautiful picture of the good news of Jesus and His body—the church—living in union just as God designed. As we close, let's let this prophecy permeate our minds and hearts:

> **The Spirit of the Sovereign Lord is upon me, for the Lord has anointed me to bring good news to the poor. He has sent me to comfort the brokenhearted and to proclaim that captives will be released and prisoners will be freed. He has sent me to tell those who mourn that the time of the Lord's favor has come, and with it, the day of God's anger against their enemies. To all who mourn in Israel, he will give a crown of beauty for ashes, a joyous blessing instead of mourning, festive praise instead of despair. In their righteousness, they will be like great oaks that the Lord has planted for his own glory. They will rebuild the ancient ruins, repairing cities destroyed long ago. They will revive them, though they have been deserted for many generations.**
>
> —Isaiah 61:1-4

We've come to the end of this journey together, but this isn't the end—it is just the beginning! You and I have become a part of the sanctuary and habitation of the very Spirit of God! We are living stones! Now is the time to live as the church and to give away what we have received.

Meditate

Jesus is in heaven reaching out His hands. His eyes are on you, and He is praying for you. He has equipped you for the work He's designed you to do. You are who He says you are, and you have all that you need to fulfill His plans.

What do you hear Jesus saying? Who is He causing your heart to hurt for?

Prayer

Father,

You have given me a new life with new purpose. You have set me on the strong rock of Jesus and now I know You as my peace and protection. I re-member what my life was like before I was joined to You, and I will never forget the mercy and grace You've shown me. Let my life be a living sacrifice for You and Your kingdom. Help me fulfill all that You've planned.

Lord, I'm united and filled with You, and we have a big family! I will serve and love the people beside me with the gifts You've given. Inspire me to love them well!

Together with Your church, I'm being built up as a part of Your Bride. Help us keep our eyes on You. Help us to ready for Your return. Permeate us with

*Your love and Your light as we shine brightly for
You — to give away what we have received.*
  Jesus, this is all for You!
  Thank You for loving me.
  I love You too.
  Amen.

Works Cited

Capps, Charles. *God's Creative Power*. Capps Publishing, 1976.

"Communion." *Cambridge Dictionary,* Cambridge Advanced Learner's Dictionary & Thesaurus © Cambridge University Press, *https://dictionary.cambridge.org/us/dictionary/english/communion.* Accessed 7 July 2020.

Frangipane, Francis. *In Christ's Image Training, Level I, Track Two: Humility, Chapter Seven Brokenness Creates Openness.* Arrow Publications Inc., 2004.

——, *In Christ's Image Training, Level I, Track Three: Prayer.* Arrow Publications Inc., 2004.

Frost, Jack. *Experiencing Father's Embrace*. Destiny Image Publishers, Inc., 2002.

Heflin, Ruth Ward. *Glory*. McDougal Publishing, 1990.

Hinn, Benny. *Good Morning, Holy Spirit*. Thomas Nelson, 1990.

Lewis, C. S. *The Weight of Glory*. HarperCollins, 1949.

Murray, Andrew. *Covenants and Blessings*. Whitaker House, 1984.

Murray, Andrew. *With Christ in the School of Prayer*. Whitaker House, 1981.

Neese, Zach. *How to Worship a King*. Gateway Create Publishing, 2015.

Redpath, Alan. *Victorious Christian Service*. Alan Redpath, 2013.

If You're a Fan of This Book, Please Tell Others...

- Post a 5-Star review on Amazon.

- Write about the book on your Facebook, Twitter, Instagram page—any social media you regularly use! #BecomingLivingStones

- If you have led the group study or participated in one using this book, share that experience too.

- If you blog, consider referencing the book, your study experiences, or publishing an excerpt from the book with a link to my website. You have my permission to do this as long as you provide proper credit and backlinks.

- Recommend the book to friends. Word-of-mouth is still the most effective form of advertising.

- Purchase additional copies to give as gifts. You can do this by visiting my website: alavishinglife.com